A
MENTOR'S
WISDOM

Dr. Haddon Robinson (1931–2017)

A MENTOR'S WISDOM

LESSONS I LEARNED FROM

HADDON ROBINSON

R. LARRY MOYER

HENDRICKSON PUBLISHERS

A Mentor's Wisdom:
Lessons I Learned from Haddon Robinson

Hendrickson Publishers Marketing, LLC
P. O. Box 3473
Peabody, Massachusetts 01961-3473
www.hendrickson.com

ISBN 978-1-68307-161-7

Printed in the United States of America

First Printing — April 2018

Cover design by Karol Bailey

This book is dedicated to Dr. Haddon Robinson's dear wife Bonnie and his two children, Torrey and Vicki. You have always made me feel like a part of your family. To you, Haddon was a husband and father. To me, he was my beloved mentor, and I am immensely grateful for what I learned through that relationship with him.

Larry, Vicki, Torrey, and Bonnie at
Dr. Robinson's memorial service (2017)

Contents

WORK COUNSEL

SPIRITUAL ADVICE

PUBLIC SPEAKING AND PREACHING

LEADERSHIP

EVANGELISM

Foreword

Every Tuesday night, the doorbell would ring. Towering, adult men would clomp into our house. They'd fill the den, spill over the sofa, fill the padded bench, and pull up all the chairs from the kitchen. Sometimes they'd plop down on the floor trying to take notes on shag carpet. They'd come eager to hear my father hold court.

I always enjoyed Tuesdays—largely because my mother would buy Southern Maid donuts. After I drove to the store with her and helped her set things up, she'd let me select whichever donut I wanted. (I stayed loyal to chocolate.) Then the doorbell would begin to "brinnng."

After greeting the men, I'd go to my room to get ready for bed. From my bedroom, I could hear my father's voice and theirs as they asked questions or exploded with occasional bursts of laughter. Those men who I considered "old", I realize now were only in their mid-twenties. They were Dallas Theological Seminary students studying to become preachers. Dad held a class in our house every Tuesday night.

While I recall those evenings in terms of donuts, camaraderie, and a feeling of security, it wasn't until decades later that I realized the impact my father had on those men's lives. Some of those Dad taught and mentored became presidents of influential Christian schools such as Moody, Wheaton, and Biola. Some became missionaries. Others pastored congregations from California to New York to Singapore to Africa. Not all of them had callings of great note, but most made a significant impact in the circles into which they were led.

After Dad died, more than nine thousand viewers watched his memorial service online. So far as we know, twenty-seven couples named their son after him and, as I write this, as recently as yesterday a former colleague wrote how her life was impacted by his display of love. Currently, a Gordon-Conwell student is writing his dissertation about Dad's life.

The question is: Why? Why did Dr. Haddon William Robinson make such a significant mark on so many? Why was he so revered?

If you know his background, then you know that the question is worth asking. From his upbringing, you might think it unlikely that he'd make a large splash in the Kingdom pool. If you look him up on Wikipedia, you'll read that he was the former president of Gordon-Conwell Theological Seminary, as well as Denver Theological Seminary, and that he was considered one of the world's foremost experts in biblical preaching. (As one youth minister put it, "God looked down and said, 'Man! That dude can *preach*!'")

My father, who grew up in the slums of New York, earned two masters' degrees (Dallas Theological Seminary and Southern Methodist University), as well as a PhD from the University of Illinois. (Dad wouldn't tell you this, but his PhD was earned with highest honors.) He excelled at a variety of positions from holding the Harold John Ockenga Distinguished Professor of Preaching to teaching homiletics (the preparation and delivery of sermons) at Dallas Theological Seminary. He also was the general director of the Christian Medical and Dental Society.

Never one to go at things halfway, Dad excelled at almost every task he attempted. In 1996, he was named in a Baylor University poll as one of the "12 Most Effective Preachers in the English Speaking World." *Christianity Today* named him in the top 10 of its "25 Most Influential Preachers of the Past 50 Years." And, in 2008, he received the E. K. Bailey "Living Legend Award." In 2010, *Preaching* magazine named him among the "25 Most Influential Preachers of the Past 25 Years."

He never sat still. When he watched TV he did sit-ups. When he was home, he'd occupy his free time with his Bible, a book, or *TIME* magazine. He was always on the lookout for a creative, clever way to win people to Christ. He hosted the TV program *Film Festival* and was the lead Bible teacher on Radio Bible Class's popular daily broadcast, *Discover the Word*, which for twenty years broadcast six hundred times daily to two million listeners throughout North America and around the world.

Dad was perhaps best known as a teacher of preachers, and he was the very best example of what he taught. He received invitations to preach somewhere around the globe almost every weekend. When he wasn't speaking, he was writing. He wrote for *Christianity Today*, *Bibliotheca Sacra*, *Moody Monthly*, *American Lutheran*, *Leadership*, and *Decision*, and for the devotional *Our Daily Bread*. He is best known, however, for his hallmark text *Biblical Preaching: The Development and Delivery of Expository Messages*, the textbook used by seminaries and Bible colleges around the world to teach students to preach the Bible in a way that's accurate, interesting, and relevant.

With all those accomplishments (and those don't include the honorary doctorates, awards, and many, many other honors), he was a man who left his thumbprints all over the lives of countless men and women. My brother Torrey and I are proud to bear those thumbprints. We would both tell you that Dad was the finest man we've ever known.

He cared about others. He would never tell you about his accomplishments. In fact, it made him very uncomfortable when people bragged on him or fussed over him. (My brother and I joke that this is not an inherited trait!) What delighted him was to build into others and to see those he mentored go on to grow God's Kingdom.

One of the choice servants bearing Dad's thumbprint is Larry Moyer. Dad encouraged Larry and believed in him at a crucial time in his life. I doubt Dad foresaw when he started working with Larry how much his encouragement and counsel would influence Larry. Nor would Dad have been able to know how Larry would use his God-given gifts along with the Dad's counsel to grow EvanTell into a ministry that would reach millions of people with the gospel of Christ.

Larry never lost his gratitude for Dad. Larry loved Dad deeply, and Dad loved Larry. Torrey and I hope that you, too, benefit from Dad's mentoring through Larry's memories of our father.

This book was written as a tribute to our dad. Hopefully, it will serve as a blessing to you. Most importantly, we hope it honors our Lord whom both Dad and Larry so faithfully gave their lives to serve.

Vicki Hitzges
Dallas, Texas
2018

February 27, 1974
Our Fiftieth Year

Dear Alumnus of Dallas Seminary. . .

Forgive this impersonal approach, but I have something to share with
you that I think may be important to your ministry. This is the
simplest way I know to tell you about it.

As a pastor, I am sure that you are interested in knowing of evangelists
who preach the clear Gospel of Jesus Christ effectively. For that
reason, I think you will be interested in Mr. Larry Moyer who is
a recent graduate of Dallas Seminary. Larry has held evangelistic meetings
throughout the United States, and God has blessed his presentation
of the Gospel in an unusual way. He has conducted church campaigns and
united campaigns, and in addition has worked effectively with young people.

Most important to me is that he preaches a clear Gospel in the power of
the Holy Spirit. I wanted to take this means to tell you about him.

If you are interested in knowing more about his ministry, he can be reached
at Encounter International, 4230 LBJ Freeway, Dallas, Texas 75234. If
I can give you added information, feel perfectly free to write to me here
at the Seminary.

I hope that the work is going well for you in your corner of the vineyard.

Warmly,

Haddon W. Robinson

P.S.   Larry often travels with his wife Tammy who is an accomplished
soloist.

HWR:tm

Preface

Little did I know the impact Dr. Robinson would have on my life.

From the day I was saved, I wanted to be an evangelist. While pursuing my masters at Dallas Theological Seminary, I was introduced to my preaching professor, Dr. Haddon Robinson. As soon as he started teaching, I said, "Wow, I want to communicate the way he does." What stood out to me was how easy he was to follow, how selective he was in his word choices, how he spoke without notes, and how well he related to his audience. I was soon going to discover that it wasn't so much the way he spoke but more importantly the way he thought.

One day in class, he said, "The people I help the most are those who come after me." I thought, "Look out, I'm coming!" That started a relationship that grew deeper by the year. If a student walked up to him after class to ask him a question, I stood near the student to see how he would answer it. I made appointments with him to talk about any question I had, whether it was about theology or life, because I could tell he loved those informal times with students and wanted to help. I was at every "brown bag" session he had on campus, even one on the tax deductions one gets as a minister. When he found out I wanted to be an evangelist, he encouraged me to start my own association. So, I gained all the advice I could from him on forming a board of directors. Whenever he spoke in chapel, I inquired about how he developed that message. I never met with him merely to talk, though. I continued to seek a relationship with him because I wanted to learn from him. The more I got to know him, the more I discovered how much there was to learn from him, and I kept coming back for more.

When you're first getting started as an evangelist, the biggest problem you have is getting connected, because no one knows who you are. When I graduated from Dallas Seminary, I was overwhelmed when Dr. Robinson said, "I want to write a letter to every one of our alumni recommending you as an evangelist." The next couple weeks I received more than twenty invitations from churches across the country to come and speak at evangelistic outreaches. I thought I had died and gone to heaven! Even better than receiving the first invite was watching the invitations keep coming.

I have often wondered why he seemed to have such confidence in me. Two things I remember him telling me was, "God has given you such gift." You can imagine what that meant coming from a man of his stature. The second was, "I can tell you have had quite a lot of speaking experience already." He was right, because by the time I got to seminary I had already spent two summers in the pulpit as an interim pastor. I sincerely believe he knew that with some experience behind me in speaking, I would relate and pick up very quickly on any advice he gave me. One more reason may be that he once said, "It is easier to start a good habit in speaking than to break a bad one." I think he wanted to help me start good habits as quickly as I could to avoid the formation of bad speaking habits.

Before I graduated in 1973 and founded EvanTell, Dr. Robinson could tell that I personally felt burdened to start my own association, loved to build concepts, and enjoyed a fair amount of administrative work. It was as a result of his insights into how to best create a well-functioning ministry, as well as God's nudges, that I founded EvanTell, a ministry characterized by clear presentations of the gospel of grace, careful handling of Scripture, and grace as the motivation for all we do in evangelism. For twenty-five years Dr. Robinson served on our board of directors, relaying helpful advice and consistently steering me in the right direction.

Through the ensuing years until his home-going on July 22, 2017, he profoundly impacted not only EvanTell but also my life. The truths he shared with me affected me in ways words cannot describe. I wrote this book to honor his legacy so others could benefit from his wise words the way I did in the areas of life, leadership, work, speaking, and evangelism.

May God use this book to encourage you in your walk with God in the same way he used Dr. Haddon Robinson to encourage me.

LIFE LESSONS

1. **"Decide now what you want people to carve on your tombstone, and then live your life backwards from there."**

   So teach us to number our days,
   That we may gain a heart of wisdom. (Ps. 90:12)

   When I was in charge of the senior retreat during my fourth year of seminary, I invited Dr. Robinson to be one of the speakers. In one of the sessions he commented, "Decide now what you want people to carve on your tombstone. Then live your life backwards from there." There is no way he could have said louder, better, or clearer, "How do you want to be remembered?"

   After spending time on my knees before the Lord, I decided the epitaph I wanted was, "Here lies a man of grace who loved sinners."

   Psalm 90 contains a prayer of Moses that discusses how short and fragile our lives are. Because we are here today and gone tomorrow, we should do our best to remember the idea behind verse 12 and be aware of our own mortality so that we can use our time for eternal purposes. That is, we should use it for the things that will have eternal importance, not the things that are perishable and will be forgotten quickly. Sooner or later, we will pass on from this life and all of our opportunities to contribute to the kingdom of God—through introducing someone to Christ, encouraging a person who has no hope for the future, using your investments for eternal causes, modeling a Christlike life before those who have never seen one, or helping a neighbor in need—will be no longer. Whatever good we want to do—whatever contribution we want to make—must be done before our lives are over; it cannot be done afterward.

I know a person who took that verse so literally that he numbered how many days he had between now and seventy (cf. v. 10) and checked off each day to remind himself how little time he had left. He wanted to make sure his remaining days were spent wisely and were making a positive impact on others' lives. In this way, his epitaph was on his mind every day.

I later learned through Dr. Robinson's daughter, Vicki, that he had thought through his own epitaph. When she once asked him how he wanted to be remembered, he answered, "I would hope people would say, 'He was held in love and high esteem by those who knew him best.'" As I interacted with those at his memorial service, they all agreed that it reflected the way his life was centered on the eternal and was a good representation of the way others viewed him.

No matter where you are in life and no matter what you are doing, you would be wise to pause and think, "What is going to be *my* epitaph?"

2. **"In the multitude of counselors there is much wisdom, but there can also be much confusion."**

Where there is no counsel, the people fall;
But in the multitude of counselors there is
*   safety. (Prov. 11:14)*

People that "rock the boat" can cause us to say, "Now wait a minute. What was done before works just fine." Usually, though, if we think about what they're saying, we are helped by it. On more than one occasion, Dr. Robinson did that for me. He said things in such a way that I thought perhaps he got his words confused. I wasn't sure I agreed with him. But every single time he caused me to think deeper.

Because he was so committed to the truth of Scripture, Dr. Robinson fulfilled what Proverbs 11:14 was saying in its entirety. His point was that we should have the right kind and number of counselors because, as he says, many voices and opinions can lead to "much confusion."

It then dawned on me that inherent in that verse were three thoughts. First, we need to go to people who know what they are talking about. Just anybody won't do. Depending on what I need advice on, I ask specific people who I know are knowledgeable in that area to guide me. Second, I should ask more than one person for their opinion and help because no one person is right all the time. I need a multitude. However, multitude doesn't always mean a hundred; in most cases it means only a few select people. Numerous perspectives can be very helpful in deciding the best way to proceed. Finally, I have to be willing to listen. If I'm not willing to listen to and consider their advice, then I shouldn't ask anyone to take the time to give me their opinion.

Years ago when our son came along, my wife, Tammy, and I outgrew the small house we had purchased after I graduated from seminary. The good news was that the house had tripled in value. But because I was inexperienced in the housing market, I wasn't sure what to do in order to be a good steward of that equity. How big of a house do I purchase? How far in debt do I go? What kind of loan do I get? In the midst of all those questions, the one thing I realized was that too many voices would have confused me, so I sought out the advice from a single banker—a man I respected in his handling of money and a wise person in the housing market. He also was one who had contact with others with the same expertise and could give me their collective wisdom. He helped me pull it all together and make a decision that would be best for my family in the long term.

Another situation in which what Dr. Robinson said affected a major decision was when my wife and I had to take the car away from my mother-in-law for both her own safety as well as the safety of others. Despite the fact that her sight and hearing were impaired, she was unwilling to give her car up. In an effort to be both sensitive and firm, we got legal advice from an attorney as well as friends of ours who had faced similar situations in their own families.

Everyone at some time or another needs counsel from wise and trustworthy people. Select those people carefully. Depending on how it's done, there can be many excellent things to learn. But beware: advice from too many people can also be overwhelming.

3. "Your children will bring you the highest of highs and the lowest of lows."

Behold, children are a heritage from the LORD, *The fruit of the womb is a reward. (Ps. 127:3)*

When you are close to your mentor, you see them from many different sides. You quickly pick up how he or she feels about life, friends, money, education, travel, politics, and a host of other items. You also learn how they feel about the people they spend the most time with—their husband or wife and children.

You did not have to be around Dr. Robinson long to know how he felt about his dear wife, Bonnie, or his children, Torrey and Vicki. His children were to him what the Bible calls them—a gift from God—and he would have done anything for them. I saw him delighted for them when things were going well, and I also watched him struggle alongside them when they faced hard times.

We were talking about the thousands of experiences he had interacting with other parents when, in his tender but honest way, he made the above comment. I appreciated his honesty that while every child is a gift of God, life with that gift can be very difficult and even painful. A child is diagnosed with cancer. A child develops the wrong kind of friends. A child is voted "most likely to succeed." A child receives the highest honor given to a graduating student. A child gets pregnant outside of wedlock. A child is the victim of a car accident. A child's spouse walks out on them. Indescribable highs. Indescribable lows. The excitement that follows the highs and the pain that comes with the lows are there when these things happen to you, but the feelings are heightened when they occur to your *own children*.

I could sense why Dr. Robinson was giving such a warning. While most parents knew the truth in his statement, it is extremely important that every new parent meditate on it in preparation for having children so they are not surprised when those times come.

His words are also a welcome reminder to parents who feel stuck in a rut feeling one way or another. When the highs and lows come, it's important to remember that neither lasts forever. Despairing, agonizing times will come, but they will always be cushioned by terrifically beautiful high moments.

4. "Life is often a choice not between the good and the bad but the good and the good."

Trust in the Lord with all your heart,
And lean not on your own understanding;
In all your ways acknowledge Him,
And He shall direct your paths. (Prov. 3:5–6)

During one of my many phone conversations with Dr. Robinson, he asked, "How are *you* doing?"

I answered, "Okay. I am just feeling a bit overwhelmed."

In his caring way, he responded, "Why's that?"

I then explained that as a result of God's abundant blessings on my evangelistic ministry, I was being given more opportunities than ever to speak at evangelistic outreaches, write articles for national magazines, attend leadership conferences as a plenary speaker, and teach evangelism at schools. I knew I could not do everything, but had no idea how I could possibly decide which ones to accept.

That is when he said, "In other words, you are trying to decide between the good and the good." I paused, struck by what he said. He then explained that in our decision making, it's easy to feel as though one choice is good and the other bad, when that could not be further from the truth. In reality, either decision would be a good one. I just had to decide which good one to make.

That's when I realized how helpful Proverbs 3:5–6 is. We need to walk with a conscious dependence upon God. If we make that a pattern of our lives, then he will direct us down the path that will allow us to best serve him. Sometimes his direction is communicated through prayer and other times through seeking the wisdom of others. Dr. Robinson even assured me that it was not wrong to list the pros and cons of different choices and decide accordingly.

I recently had to decline an invitation to speak at a Bible college for a week. It was not an easy decision. While I recognize that I was turning down an excellent opportunity to train others in evangelism, at the same time, I was able to speak at an evangelistic outreach where many came to Christ. After carefully thinking through the two options, I decided to choose the outreach. What helped stem my guilt and frustration at not being able to fulfill the needs of both options were Dr. Robinson's words. In the end, God's plan for those students at the college didn't end with my dismissal of the opportunity; they would find someone else to preach what needed to be said. Even more importantly, neither choice was the wrong one; I was deciding between the good and the good. Decisions like those allow me to truly listen for God's voice and calling.

When faced with similar decisions, remember to free yourself up. Don't look at every decision as a good or bad one. Be grateful for good choices, walk in humble dependence upon God, and let him direct you.

5. "I'll tell you one thing: That book is alive."

For the word of God is living and powerful, and sharper than any two-edged sword, piercing even to the division of soul and spirit, and of the joints and marrow, and is a discerner of the thoughts and intents of the heart. (Heb. 4:12)

During one of my Doctor of Ministry classes taught by Dr. Robinson at Gordon-Conwell Theological Seminary, Dr. Robinson looked as though he had a powerful thought about the Bible and wanted to tell us. With that characteristic index finger pointed our way, he said in a most emphatic tone, "I'll tell you one thing: That book is *alive*." I found myself deeply impacted by his statement because I had just finished an in-depth study of Hebrews 4:12.

During my study of the verse, I realized that I had been taking that verse too lightly. Similar to the emphasis in Dr. Robinson's words, the Scriptures stress their truly penetrating powers to the point where they are stronger and greater than even the most intimidating, piercing weapons: a double-edged sword. The Bible cuts into the inner recesses of our spiritual being, able to divide the soul and spirit. It can tell us what our motivations are and whether they are of the flesh or the spirit.

That's why we often feel convicted, sometimes to the point of tears, when we read the word with an open and teachable spirit. One sentence can change our entire lives. Perhaps that is why one person I know put a note on the cover of his Bible that read, "Danger: Open at your own risk!"

A verse that has significantly impacted my life and the way I live every day is John 5:24. It reminds me that, having trusted Christ, I have eternal life. Anyone who has come to the Savior will never be condemned, because their admission of sin and guilt allows them to pass from death into life. Eternal life is my present possession, not something I receive after I die. What a thrill to get out of bed every morning realizing that I have already begun to live eternally. No verse of the Bible excites me more than this one does.

In addition, I have been impacted by the book of Proverbs. Along with studying a book of the Bible each morning, I read the chapter of Proverbs that corresponds to that day—the sixth Proverb on the sixth day of the month, and so on. The first time I came across Proverbs 30:8b–9, I thought, "How did I miss that before?" The passage reads,

> Give me neither poverty nor riches
> Feed me with the food allotted to me;
> Lest I be full and deny You,
> And say, "Who is the LORD?"
> Or lest I be poor and steal,
> And profane the name of my God.

I did not desire poverty, but the verse took away any desire for riches. Throughout my life, I have seen first-hand the accuracy of that passage. Some are able to wisely manage their riches or are content in their poverty. However, more often than not I have met people whose riches—or lack thereof—control them.

Reading that verse again with fresh eyes was the key to truly being able to soak in the words and apply them to my life. My renewed awareness of the verse also proves that the Bible will surprise us and touch our hearts when we're least expecting it. We should never discount the Bible's ability to impact us. Therefore, let's continue digging into the word with the knowledge that God will bring certain passage to our attention when we need to hear it or put it into practice.

In the spirit of the Bible's powerful content, keep your eyes open and heart ready, because you never know when it may be relevant to you. Beware: The book you are opening is alive!

6. "Aging is not for sissies."

Do not cast me off in the time of old age;
Do not forsake me when my strength
*   fails. (Ps. 71:9)*

For many years after I graduated, I saw Dr. Robinson at least once or twice a year and would frequently speak with him on the phone when he served on EvanTell's board of directors. Then, when I decided to get my Doctor of Ministry degree in Business Ethics and Leadership in the Workplace, I was back in Dr. Robinson's classroom at Gordon-Conwell more than thirty years after I first met him. Since I had to be on campus for a couple weeks each year for three years but could study the rest of the time was off campus, I could maintain my traveling schedule as an evangelist.

In that class, he stressed that one cannot be a leader unless one can communicate. So, he gave us an assignment to come up with a five-minute talk wrapped around a central idea. On our assignment's due date, he surprised us by giving us his own talk before we gave ours.

As he gave his five-minute talk, as usual his choice of words gripped me. What I could not miss was his main idea: "Aging is not for sissies" (based on a quote from actress Bette Davis). He proved it by talking about the battles he had to face as his strength faded and his eyes dimmed, and the difference in his physical physique from thirty years ago. With transparency, he spoke of the coming time when he would have to close his wife's eyelids in death or she would have to close his.

In order to deal with that painful reality, he stressed that the best form of preparation was just to accept it. We are not going to be able to do some of the things we used to do. We need to be willing to let others help us without feeling ashamed or offended. We will have to make plans for our departures so our families are not in a state of confusion when we pass. That is one reason Dr. Robinson and Bonnie moved to an assisted living place in Lancaster, Pennsylvania, as his strength started to fail. He wanted to help his children prepare for their passing. We must face the fact that the years we have left are rapidly diminishing.

Having trusted in the Lord his entire life, the psalmist did not want God to dismiss him in his old age. He did not want his enemies to conclude that God had forsaken him. What particularly penetrates my heart are the emotions present in the paragraph. The psalmist felt the agony of aging. The longevity of life had taken its toll on his health and strength.

We ought not to tease ourselves with the hope that our youth will last forever. Our strength will fail, and our hearing and eyesight will diminish. Our minds will not be as sharp. Facing those realities will not be easy, but preparing for them helps. Preparation will lead us to acceptance and will open doors to learn how to best deal with it.

7. "Never make decisions in the midst of a mood."

Ponder the path of your feet,
And let all your ways be established. (Prov. 4:26)

In another one of those small group settings, Dr. Robinson was leaning back in his chair in a reflective mood when, with his graceful forthrightness, he gave the above caution. He explained that emotions cannot be trusted. Our feelings are often the result of the human spirit, not the Holy Spirit, and hence can blur our judgment. It is better to wait until those emotions subside and we can think more rationally. He was not saying that emotions are wrong. He was saying that when they are used in decision making, they can be dangerous. That caused me to reflect on my own decision making and his wise advice. There are times I make decisions out of excitement. When the excitement is over, I wonder if I thought through the decision to the degree I should have. Excitement is not the only emotion that can stifle someone's rationality, though. There is danger in deciding something out of sadness, anger, jealousy, and more.

Years ago, I had an opportunity to go on a hunt in the Northwest. Being an avid hunter, I readily accepted without doing my homework. I later learned that it was not the best situation, because I did not share the same priorities as the person I was hunting with. Looking back, I had initially reacted out of emotion and ended up in a situation that made me uncomfortable.

An example that comes to mind was when a friend of mine bought a large piece of property without thinking through the potential ramifications. A short time later, it cost him his marriage.

What could one lose by letting the emotions pass before making a decision? Dr. Robinson's counsel was "Nothing." After letting the feelings of the moment simmer down, common sense enters in, allowing one to think intelligently, measure the pros and cons, and exercise sound judgment.

Proverbs 4:26 reinforces Dr. Robinson's caution. The passage highlights the importance of wisdom— something far more trustworthy than emotion. Something to remember, though, is that wisdom can include emotion and those emotions can be helpful. However, the context is time and thoughtfulness. To "ponder" means to carefully weigh our steps with calm and serious thinking. This intentionality leads to sound decisions and assurance that you won't be tripped up by unforeseen ramifications. Time spent thinking about and analyzing the best response helps you make the best possible decision. Emotions can help or hinder. Regardless, they should not solely guide us.

8. "Make it a point to speak a word of praise to someone once each day."

Therefore comfort each other and edify one another, just as you also are doing. (1 Thess. 5:11)

Anyone who knew Dr. Robinson could tell you what an excellent professor he was. But I think they would also tell you that their favorite times were when they interacted with him after class. If his teaching was the cake, then those times when he was able to answer questions "off the cuff" were the icing on the cake!

What made Dr. Robinson so unique, though, was that he not only taught others, he learned from them. He was touched by someone he knew who regularly gave good books to friends. Another time when he was in seminary, he and Bonnie were strapped for money and didn't know where money for the next meal was coming from. But one day they went out to their mailbox and found $25 from an anonymous giver. As he met others who consistently showed such overwhelming generosity and kindness, he admitted that it was they who taught him how to do the same for others. I believe it was through moments like those that inspired him to be gracious and complimentary of others.

While discussing one of my sermons, he observed and complimented my use of humor. Coming from a person who had such talent when it came to preaching, I was deeply touched. What makes his above advice—and his compliment of me—so meaningful is that praise is not often received. Managers are quick to be told when they do wrong and seldom complimented for doing right. Employees receive letters only if they are insensitive and rude. Few friendly and servant-minded ones get letters of praise.

There is hardly a better way to practice the exhortation of 1 Thessalonians 5:11 than to heed Dr. Robinson's suggestion. "Edify" connotes the idea of "build up." What better way to build someone up than to speak a word of praise to them? People say, "Be careful to practice what you preach." That sentence always amuses me because Paul does such a good job of doing just that. He tells the Thessalonian believers what to do and then, while telling them, does it himself! He builds them up by telling them to keep doing what they are doing.

Not long after receiving Dr. Robinson's encouragement, I returned from a funeral service. A relative who stood by the casket of a loved one had remarked, "I wish I had told her how thoughtful she was and how important she always made me feel." I left that service with a newfound passion to say whatever praise I had for someone while they were still living. I now regularly write letters or make phone calls to compliment someone for what they have done for me or a kindness I witnessed them showing to someone else.

As Dr. Robinson modeled, I encourage you to speak a word of praise to someone daily. You may be surprised how much you're already inclined to look for the good in others. You may also be surprised how much good there is to find!

9. "Time is your enemy. You must work to make it your friend."

To everything there is a season,
A time for every purpose under heaven. (Eccl. 3:1)

Some people teach on such a theoretical level that it is difficult to know how to apply what they are saying. I know a woman who struggled to forgive her ex-husband for walking out on her after more than twenty years of marriage. She was told, "You have to forgive and forget." She found herself frustrated, thinking, "How do you forget what actually happened? It will always be there and has had major effects on my life." I explained to her that forgetting does not mean it never comes to your mind. What it should mean is that every time it comes to your mind, you no longer hold it against the person and you no longer dwell on it.

Part of the reason Dr. Robinson ministered to me so deeply was because of his realistic view of life, especially when it came to practical advice like that. Dr. Robinson was one of those who helped me look at things realistically, not theoretically. A good example of this is when he explained that time works against everyone. We wish for it to pause and just let us finish something we otherwise couldn't or we stare at the clock, willing it to speed up and get us through unwanted hours. Regardless of what we do, the clock keeps ticking. Absolutely nothing will change that.

The writer of Ecclesiastes states that on this sphere on which we live, there is a time for every human activity. One of the reasons for the section is to remind us that we have control over some moments in time, but most we don't. Dr. Robinson's exhortation was to make a friend out of the small part we do have control over.

How do we do this? We follow Dr. Robinson's example: Decide what can reasonably be achieved in a given amount of time and what can't. Plan three hours for a project that may take only two. Intentionally direct the activities of our days to the best of our abilities instead of letting them overwhelm us. Prioritize the things that need to get done and take out whatever can be done later. Practice patience and endurance when we feel time pressing in on us or when we are in a moment that we wish would end. Make changes in our schedules so we can be as efficient as possible, making time work for us, not against us. We should aim to get to a place where we no longer dread, or even look at, the clock. In other words, we need to take control of time in the ways we can. In so doing, we are being good stewards of our time and we can rest knowing that we're using every sliver to our advantage.

One time a friend said to me, "Larry, you are always telling me what you have put into your schedule. You never tell me what you have taken out." I appreciated the practicality of what his statement implied: by explaining what we are taking out of our schedule, we gain an acute awareness of what our choices suggest for our time. We have to be conscious of what we take out of our schedule as well as what that means for the activities we leave in. Through doing that, time becomes our friend with whom we can talk and reason, instead of an all-encompassing tyrant.

10. "There are two kinds of people: Those who pass through experiences and experienced people."

A wise man will hear and increase learning,
And a man of understanding will attain
*   wise counsel. (Prov. 1:5)*

I come from a background where transparency was not encouraged. Even hugging someone and telling them "I love you" was difficult. There were those I knew loved me. But none of them actually said to me, "I love you." I wasn't around people who shared their deepest hurts and feelings, so I assumed people didn't do that. I never wanted anyone to see me with a tear in my eye. Big boys don't cry, do they? Intimate subjects such as sex were never discussed. I had to learn how to share my deepest thoughts and feelings with others, and it wasn't an easy road. Even in ministry, when a new convert gave me the biggest hug because of the part I played in leading him to Christ, I felt awkward.

The more comfortable I became with Dr. Robinson, the more I opened up to him. I am a bit surprised I did because of how uncomfortable I felt doing that with anyone. As I reflect back, there were two things that helped. First, I always sensed that when Dr. Robinson asked "How are you doing?" he meant it. His words and demeanor breathed sincerity. Second, he led me to do so by example. He opened up to me and shared some of his own hurts and feelings. On one occasion, his speaking did not go as well as he had hoped. Looking back, he felt it was because he had misread his audience.

In one of those times, I shared an experience where I wished I had done something differently. In a particular message I gave, I chose the wrong illustrations and came away feeling that the people endured my speaking instead of enjoying or learning from it. After I told him the story, he encouraged and taught me by making the above statement. He explained that there are people who go through one experience after another. That may seem natural, but that is *all* they do. They never learn from those experiences. Proverbs teaches that a wise person never stops learning. People who want to learn let experiences teach them something and apply what they have learned to future interactions and opportunities. They go into the next experience wiser by altering their approach to and outlook on life. Consistently they welcome wise counsel.

You incurred a debt that should not have been incurred. Did you learn from the experience or simply acquire another debt?

You were hasty in your judgment of another. What did you learn about being slower to cast judgment?

You promised too much to too many. Do you keep doing it or do you now say "no" when necessary?

You are consistently late to your appointments. Is your excuse "That's just me," or have you learned to be on time?

Our day-to-day experiences are priceless. They are tools God uses to teach us. We are helped only when we choose to excavate the valuable lessons present in every moment.

11. "Temperament is not holy. Don't be afraid to make impulsive decisions when you need to."

So God created man in His own image; in the image of God He created him; male and female He created them. (Gen. 1:27)

It was another one of those "in the car" conversations (it seems like we had quite a few of those) when I shared with Dr. Robinson that I had discovered some new things about myself: I am a slow processor and make the best decisions when I have time to ponder them. I don't need days, but even having overnight helps. The three things that help me the most as I process are people, prayer, and time. In response, he affirmed that my habits were strengths and would keep me from making hasty choices. However, he also cautioned me not to let that strength become a weakness. As he made the above statement, he forewarned me that there will be times I would *have* to make impulsive decisions, and I should not be afraid to do so when the moment arose.

We began to discuss the temperaments one comes across in ministry and how people's personalities affect their approach to evangelism and how quickly they make decisions. That conversation led to a discussion about how people look at their personalities and temperaments as being perfect and holy, using them as an excuse to get out of doing what they need to do. In other words, sometimes it's not the length of time that hinders a good choice, but instead our personalities and mind-sets because we shy away from decisions that force us out of our comfort zone. He simply wanted me to be constantly aware of the times in leadership I would be tempted to use my comfort zone in waiting to make a decision to obstruct the best path forward. Sometimes we should make an impulsive decision, or go against our typical response, and not be afraid to do so, for the sake of the situation.

Genesis speaks of us being made in God's image. As people created by him, we have the ability to communicate and respond to him—things that mark him mark us such as life, personality, thoughts, and love. We have the ability to sympathize with others, put ourselves in others' shoes, and think critically about life, our problems, and our relationships with others. However, even though God crafted each and every one of us in our mother's wombs, this does not make us perfect or free us from our own sinfulness. As a result of the fall, we are flawed and finite, and our personalities have holes and failings mingled throughout them. There are times we have to act outside of our comfort zones, just as when I have to make impulsive decisions. We cannot let our temperaments hold us back from doing whatever is necessary.

A hurricane once caused the cancellation of a major speaking engagement in Texas, four days prior to the event. A month later, the opportunities to squeeze them back into my schedule arose. If I decided to preach that day, it would severely complicate several commitments I had already made to others, to the point where I would have to ask them to reschedule as well. While I wanted time to think it through more, I just didn't have it. A decision was needed then. There was no time to process slowly!

There is no room in God's design of human beings for us to say, "I cannot help it. That is just the way I am." It is true that there are strengths in the way we think, act, and what we prefer. But we must remember that uncontrolled strengths can become a weakness. Our temperaments are not holy. We must be willing to change when necessary.

12. "This Parkinson's is rough. But the people here are great and the food is good."

And we know that all things work together for good to those who love God, to those who are the called according to His purpose. (Rom. 8:28)

When I got the news not long after I had received my Doctor of Ministry degree in 2009, I called him. I assured him of my prayers as I told him I how regretful I was that he had been diagnosed with Parkinson's disease. He told me the doctors informed him it would take its toll in about five years.

What struck me when I hung up the phone was that he had no complaints. No questioning of God's ways. No bitterness. No anger.

When I later went to see him in Lancaster, Pennsylvania, I knew it would not be easy. For the first time I would be pushing him in his wheelchair. When I arrived, he spoke briefly of how difficult Parkinson's disease was. Then it seemed he wanted to get off that subject. He spoke of how kind those were around him and how grateful he was for good food. He seemed more concerned about knowing how I was doing and what was happening at EvanTell. As I left, I thought, "I have heard Romans 8:28 all my life, but here is a person who is actually living out the verse." We are assured that no matter what comes into our lives, God will use it to make to conform us to the image of his Son. God has a plan and whatever happens, he will take care of us. While so many of us have that verse memorized in our hearts, it's baffling how few of us remember that or live like that when life sends us a bombshell.

I often ask myself, "What made Dr. Robinson so positive in the midst of such a painful and horrible disease?" One reason, as his own family remarked, was that he had such a deep faith in God. He saw God as a person who was too loving to do us wrong and too wise to make a mistake. A second reason I sensed is that he believed so deeply in the cross! A God who loves us enough to die as our substitute would never desire to harm us. Painful disease is part of being in a fallen world.

We sing the Lord's praises when life is right side up. Could we sing them when life turns upside down? Are we simply quoting Romans 8:28, or are we living it?

WORK COUNSEL

13. "I want to be on your team, not on your back."

And when Saul had come to Jerusalem, he tried to join the disciples; but they were all afraid of him, and did not believe that he was a disciple. But Barnabas took him and brought him to the apostles. And he declared to them how he had seen the Lord on the road, and that He had spoken to him, and how he had preached boldly at Damascus in the name of Jesus. (Acts 9:26–27)

The spirit Dr. Robinson had in being such an encourager always endeared him to me. He once wrote me a note that said, "I really appreciate you, Larry. I appreciate the gifts that God has given you and the splendid work that you are doing for our Savior as an evangelist." I felt he was on my team regardless of whether I succeeded or failed. Without fail, he showed immense understanding when I discussed the pressure I felt with my workload, and he always tried to relieve it instead of adding to it.

His spirit reminded me of Barnabas in the Scriptures. It is understandable why the disciples were cautious about Paul and wondered if his conversion was real. What is most honorable is how Barnabas, with his gift of encouragement, defended Paul before the apostles and proved himself to be a loyal supporter. I know people who stated that if they ever fell into any type of sin, Dr. Robinson would be the first one to whom they would run because of his accepting, supportive spirit like that of Barnabas. They knew he'd help them get back on track. Dr. Robinson always genuinely wanted to know how he could help you get through even the toughest scenarios.

One time Dr. Robinson supported me was during my last year of seminary when I had been chosen by my classmates as one of the best preachers of our class. Therefore, during Senior Preachers Week at Dallas Seminary, I was one of the four preachers who spoke that week.

After my "senior sermon" in chapel, I walked into Dr. Robinson's office. He looked at me and said, "God has given you such gift. I just wish you knew where to place your tongue for certain sounds." I asked, "What did you just say?" He repeated his comment. Fighting back tears, I said, "Dr. Robinson, I've never had anyone tell me that. I've been told I'm lazy when I speak." Knowing my strong work ethic, he chuckled and said, "You're the last guy I'd call lazy." Without hesitation or doubt in my speaking abilities, he managed to understand one of my most difficult struggles: an inherited speech defect that was so severe that I could not pronounce the word "the." While my own doctor told me that I could never be a public speaker, Dr. Robinson affirmed my choice to persevere through this issue by referring me to Beverlee Warren, a speech therapist and committed believer. Knowing speech, she instantly knew what I had been born with and was surprised how far I had come. I shared my testimony about that day in high school when I told God, "If you will heal me of this impediment, I'll always use my voice for you." She was convinced that she could take me the rest of the way, and met with me every other week for a year to retrain my tongue where to go for certain sounds.

I was able to conquer my speech defect because one man, Dr. Robinson, was on my team, not my back. While others criticized my speaking abilities and questioned my gift, he never stopped being there for me when I needed him.

How about you? When others do wrong, are you in their corner or in their face? When someone makes a poor decision, do you embrace them or embarrass them? If they are feeling the weight of life's load, do you make it lighter? If they need help getting back on track, do they sense your scorn or your support? These are critical questions to answer because they determine whether they need your assistance or just someone to be there for them. What a reward it is to help someone get to a place they may have never arrived at without you.

14. "If something is worth doing, it is worth doing poorly. However, pity the person who does not know when he has to do it well."

And whatever you do, do it heartily, as to the Lord and not to men. (Col. 3:23)

When Dr. Robinson said that (based on G. K. Chesterton's famous quote), it was the only thing I could think about for days afterward. At the time, I was graduating from seminary and doing my best to build my speaking invitations. I found myself struck by his diversion from the classic saying, "If something is worth doing, it is worth doing well." As he recognized, you cannot put the same amount of time and effort into everything you do. In an attempt to put his advice to work, I challenged myself to decide what classes I should strive for an A in. Doing this helped me recalibrate my focus back onto the topics and classes that would be of the most importance to my future ministry. Once I graduated, putting his advice into motion also helped me decide which events I need to spend more time preparing for. It became obvious that I should put in more hours of study and preparation for major evangelistic events than for fiftieth wedding anniversary speeches and toasts.

While it is true that you have to do your tasks as unto the Lord, not unto men, as a person responsible for being a good steward of your time, you have to evaluate your plate and decide what is more worthy of your time and attention.

As I got to know Dr. Robinson and looked back over what he had done and his classes, I could clearly see where he adhered to this principle. At one point when we met as a class at his home, I could tell that though he took his teaching very seriously, this time he had not prepared with the same effort he had put into other classes because the group was small and more informal. Because he knew that we were not expecting or demanding an intense outline of discussion points, he wisely chose not to fuss over creating it.

By the same token, right after EvanTell got started, we asked Dr. Robinson to write a booklet that explained the way we as a ministry were approaching evangelistic preaching. While at first he agreed, he later came back and asked if he could decline. His reasoning was that the booklet demanded "first-class effort," and because he was so overwhelmed, he recognized that he could not give it that.

Have you been asked to assist with two major events at the church? Don't treat them of equal importance if they aren't. If given responsibility with a community project, what part of it demands your best and what part of it doesn't? When planning a family outing, it would be nice to have everything planned perfectly, but does it really matter if it isn't when work responsibilities demand greater priority? If two writing projects are in front of you, what are their purposes, audiences, and impacts? Should that not determine the kind of effort you give them? If fulfilling a friend's request, does the friend really care if it is the best you can do? We must do everything as unto the Lord. But, as Dr. Robinson recognized, that does not mean everything deserves the same priority. We must discern what must be done well and what can, rightfully, be given less effort. Only then can we be proper stewards of our time. In everything we do, we must decide what deserves a first-class effort. But we must also decide what doesn't.

15. "I have learned to put everything that happens in my life in a minor or major column. What has surprised me is how few major items there are."

"Therefore do not worry about tomorrow, for tomorrow will worry about its own things. Sufficient for the day is its own trouble." (Matt. 6:34)

Part of what made Dr. Robinson's mentoring so effective is that he not only spoke from a thorough knowledge of the Scriptures, but also from his life experiences. He was quick to admit things he personally had to learn, and this transparency touched me.

There are times I saw him deeply moved by difficult situations he had to deal with, but nothing seemed to unravel him—not even the things that would unravel most people. He knew what it meant to take a day at a time and rely on God for strength.

For example, one day I walked into his home when he was looking over a bill he had just received for his son's college expenses. I could tell he was a bit stressed because he was also caring for an aging parent, and at that time faculty salaries could not support both of those financial burdens. What I admired and appreciated was how he never tried to cover up his true feelings, yet was in no way out of control of his emotions. He was putting to work his own words by not letting his circumstances affect his treatment of others or his perspective on how they affected his life.

It wasn't until he made the above comment that I began to understand how he managed to do that. The practicality of his words arrested me because I was at a point in my life where, upon reflection, things that I had considered "major" were not as major as I thought they were. I realized that Dr. Robinson had shone a bright light on what worry-free living is all about: knowing how to relegate things to the right column. God wants us to cast even the big things in life on his shoulders (1 Pet. 5:7). What helps, though, is realizing how few big things there are. College expenses in the long term are a minor issue, compared to having a mate diagnosed with terminal cancer. A "fender bender" is of concern, but seeing a house go up in flames would be much more concerning. A child who procrastinates should concern us, but not necessarily as much as a child spending time in prison.

Matthew 6:34 is a favorite of many. Unfortunately, many miss the context; the passage assures us that if God takes care of his creation—like the birds of the air and lilies in the fields—he will also take care of us, his children. While we certainly ought to be concerned about things such as food, water, and clothing, we cannot let those things become all we think about. If God takes care of birds and lilies that do not serve and love him as humans do, then he will also meet our needs.

With all that—and more—in mind, we can develop that kind of mind-set by asking ourselves, as problems arise, "How big is this, really?" Then we should put each one in the right column. With thoughtful contemplation, our minds will put all our problems in perspective, and we'll begin to see that others have faced issues that are far more major than ours. This shift helps us recognize that while something may change our weeks, our circumstances are not life-changing. Put your worries about what has happened in light of what *could* have happened. Enjoy each day by putting everything in the right column and refreshing your perspective on each issue. I think you'll find, as Dr. Robinson did, that most things aren't as major as they initially feel.

16. "There are times I have had too much to do and times I have had too little to do. Too much is definitely better."

She watches over the ways of her household,
And does not eat the bread of idleness.
(Prov. 31:27)

Around the time that Dr. Robinson stated the above comment, the demands on my schedule were building. My plate was the fullest it had ever been. So was Dr. Robinson's—even more so. He had seminary responsibilities, speaking engagements, and radio ministry, all while remaining a devoted husband and father. That's when he made the above observation.

As I reflected about what Dr. Robinson said, I realized that the Bible gives more warning to the one who has too little to do than the one who has too much to do. Anyone who reads Proverbs 31:17 knows it is talking about the characteristics of a virtuous wife. She knows how to care for her husband and family and doesn't shirk her responsibilities within the home. Not only that, the paragraph includes, "She extends her hands to the poor, yes, she reaches out her hands to the needy" (v. 20). In other words, she is not merely slaving away in the home. She is interacting with and making an impact on society. The passage adds, "She makes fine linens and sells them, and supplies sashes for the merchants." Her family members aren't the only people on her mind. As one reads what she does, one could say, "Here is a person who has too much to do." The list made me wonder how she could do it all. But what comes most clearly from the chapter is that not only does she have no time to be idle but she has no *desire* for it. This woman would far rather have too much to do, because it is in her actions and deeds that she worships God and impacts the world. The chapter closes by noting her as a person to be praised by her family and, more importantly, by God.

As I thought about the times I had too little to do, I realized those were not the times that challenged me to use my time wisely, nor were they the times that distracted me from wrong thoughts, pushed me out of my comfort zone, or stretched me mentally and emotionally. Busyness is an excellent excuse to learn how to delegate, prioritize, and assess how much time certain projects deserve. I will never have everything figured out, so busyness is also a great opportunity for me to ask God for wisdom and seek the advice of those who have gone ahead of me.

There are times when we should downsize our tasks and responsibilities because we have committed ourselves to too much. It is better to do that, though, than to wonder what there is to do. Other times, pushing through, doing as much as we possibly can, and leaving the rest to another day is the only option. If we are stuck in that scenario, we should remind ourselves that it is through these situations that we grow the most and are the most productive. We ought not to try to do more than is humanly possible, but a full plate can certainly be a signal of holy productivity, both spiritually and practically.

17. "Remember: When I recommend you, I am putting my reputation on the line."

A good name is to be chosen rather than great riches,
Loving favor rather than silver and gold.
(Prov. 22:1)

Before I talk about Dr. Robinson's quote, I'd like to share a little more about my faith journey. I was born and raised on a dairy farm in Pennsylvania. Dad told me that if I worked hard all year I could have November off to go hunting. I did not have to rush to the barn to help milk the cows after coming home from school. Instead, every day I could hit the woods. I became an avid hunter. As I observed the deer, the squirrels, the bark of the tree, and the shape of the clouds I thought, "There has to be a God." Design meant love to me, and love meant presence: a God who loved enough to create that design. I asked myself, "How do I find him? How do I get to know him?" I decided I would study the Bible. I figured that since it is God's book, it might help me. As I read, I came to understand that Christ was my only way to heaven. One night, I knelt by my bed and said, "God, the best I know how, I am trusting Christ to save me." My life exploded. As I grew as a Christian, I realized what God had done—he had led me from his creation to the creator and then to Christ.

From the day I was saved, I could not think of anything more thrilling than to be an evangelist, sharing with people everywhere God's truth. I was enamored with 2 Timothy 4:5 where Paul says to Timothy, "Do the work of an evangelist." In my spirit, I knew that was what God wanted me to pursue full time.

Getting started is not easy. People do not know you. I was overwhelmed with gratitude when, during my last year at Dallas Theological Seminary, Dr. Robinson told me, "I want to write a letter to every one of our alumni recommending you as an evangelist." Through scenarios like that one, God proved this was the path I was meant to take. Invitations kept coming years later as a result of his recommendation.

After telling me that he'd recommend me, Dr. Robinson gave me the above caution. The seriousness on his face added to it. Nothing could have shaken me any harder. Since he was a man held in such high esteem, I was horrified at the idea that I could do something that would hurt his good name.

The message of Proverbs 22:1 is unmistakable. Reputation is of more value than any wealth one owns. Money cannot buy a person's good name or favor. Someone arrives at those by the development of character, not an increased amount of possessions. A good name is priceless.

Dr. Robinson made me realize that I could hurt his good name through my own misdeeds. I could cause others to say, "I wonder why Dr. Robinson recommended *him*. I thought he had better judgment than that. Maybe Dr. Robinson is not the man I always esteemed him to be." Bad actions can not only hurt your reputation, but also the reputation of others who endorse you or have spoken highly of you. When you fall, you will take others down with you. How many ministries have greatly suffered or even folded because of the shameful actions of one person? Don't let that person be you.

SPIRITUAL ADVICE

18. "When you go through hard times, God does not promise answers. He promises himself."

*Yea, though I walk through the valley
   of the shadow of death,
I will fear no evil;
For You are with me;
Your rod and Your staff, they comfort me.
    (Ps. 23:4)*

What made Dr. Robinson's comment so impactful is that I had already spent several years in ministry. As I counseled those going through difficult situations, they often longed to know the reason behind their situation. They'd ask, "Why am I going through this? Why did God allow this to happen? What is God trying to do to me?" I cannot blame them for wondering why. As we go through hard times, who of us does not yearn for an explanation?

Dr. Robinson's point was that the "why" is not promised. What is promised is something bigger and better. That something is actually someone: the Lord. It is his presence we can count on and that makes all the difference.

One of my dearest friends suffered the loss of his wife very suddenly and unexpectedly. But even though her death was devastating, he told me, "There is nothing that substitutes for a close walk with God."

Even though Christ was not there physically, he *was* there, and my friend was imbued with the strength to go on when he didn't necessarily want to. He told me, "Two ways God has helped me through this painful time is by giving me the strength to put one foot in front of the other before I walk into my empty house, and providing you, Larry, to meet with me to help me through this grief."

Another friend, who went from golfing nationally to lying flat on his back for seven years before his passing, told me, "I don't know when the Lord has been any more real to me than through this situation." He told me that he never felt he would be able to handle life if it meant lying on his back every day, but that it seemed like each day he woke up to a fresh supply of patience. Sometimes when he was in his lowest moments a friend would walk into the room and say just the thing he needed to hear. He was given no answers, but the person and presence of Christ presented itself to him through the encouragement of loved ones.

That realization is the truth contained in Psalm 23:4. The shepherd led his sheep through dangerous passes and protected them from hidden snakes and formidable wolves. Despite the treacherous nature of the journey, all the sheep knew that the shepherd was there and that he would watch over them, making sure they wouldn't be harmed. With his rod, the shepherd could club any animal that endangered his sheep. With his staff, he pulled branches out of their way or pull a sheep out of the hole in which it had fallen.

Though maybe not in so literal a way, Christ as our shepherd does the same for us. When an injury that caused us to be laid off work created bills we were not able to pay, he provides us with the money we need from an unexpected source. Round the clock care was suddenly needed for an aging parent, with no one available until a person available for one year stepped up to the plate and offered to help. Carefully made plans for the weekend were blown out the window, causing us great frustration. In retrospect, though, that weekend was such a comfort when our best friend ended up needing our support and attention at that exact moment.

Our comfort is not in discovering the reason behind our painful circumstances; it is in the who: Christ himself. Whatever the situation, he will be there and he will get us through it, providing us with exactly what we need at precisely the right time. Sometimes it is through a friend, a letter, a powerful prayer, or just the timing of what happened that can give us peace and the knowledge that everything is in God's hands and that he is shepherding us down our best path.

In 1979, I was going on a weekend outreach in Connecticut. Through the courtesy of a free ticket I won through an American Airlines campaign, my wife was able to join me on the trip. On the second day of the outreach, the owner of the home where we were staying woke me at midnight to tell me that there was an emergency phone call for me. I received the tragic news that my father-in-law had just been killed in a car accident. Never did I think that I would have to tell my dear wife that her father had just suffered such a horrible death. What a gift it was that we were together when we got the news. Even more than that, what a gift it was that Jesus was there too. As we flew back to Dallas, we didn't have answers, but we had Jesus.

Dr. Robinson is right. It is not having answers that make the difference. Most of the time we will never get them. But we have the Lord's comforting presence and protective rod and staff! What matters is that God promises himself.

19. **"Every day you have a decision to make: You can either respond the way you had to in your old nature, or the way you've been freed up to in your new nature."**

And do not present your members as instruments of unrighteousness to sin, but present yourselves to God as being alive from the dead, and your members as instruments of righteousness to God.
(Rom. 6:13)

Not everyone can take struggles that are complex and make them understandable. However, Dr. Robinson had a way of doing just that. What helped his listeners view things differently were his word choices; he used terms people understood as well as stated things in a way others could relate to easily. I once asked him how he did that and he answered, "I work on it with every conversation I have." That is probably one reason why his answers were marked by pauses before he spoke.

The struggle between the two natures in the believer always confused me. I have heard the explanation, "There are two dogs fighting inside of you. One dog represents your old nature; the other dog represents your new nature. The one that wins the fight is the one you say 'sic 'em' to." However, the whole metaphor was quite confusing to me. Wasn't the "old dog"—in other words, my unredeemed, sinful patterns of life—dead as soon as I became a Christian? If that wicked person I used to be is still there, what was I to do with him? If our old nature is supposed to be "dead" as Romans 6:13 says, then what would saying "sic 'em" to a "live" dog do to the "dead" dog? I was familiar with Ephesians 2:1, where Paul spoke of us being "dead in trespasses and sin" prior to salvation, and I knew that because I had been saved by Christ I could now live a different, better kind of life. However, I had a hard time fully comprehending the idea that our sinful habits and thoughts are still very much a threat to our redeemed selves, because we are all sinful and always will be.

It was when Dr. Robinson and I were discussing the Bible's idea of our old natures versus how we are supposed to live now that it all came together for me. What he said helped bring the whole concept down to a level I could understand. Ultimately, he explained that following Christ and doing the right thing is a choice we all must continue to make—not just one time, when we make the decision to trust Christ as our Savior, but also daily and even hourly. It was never about uncontrollable, rampaging dogs; it is about deliberately turning our hearts away from our sinful tendencies and toward God.

Ephesians 2:2 tells us, "In which you once walked according to the course of this world, according to the prince of the power of the air, the spirit who now works in the sons of disobedience." Simply put, in our unsaved conditions, we were slaves of sin. Before we know and follow Christ, we do not have the power to turn away from our sin because we are fully immersed in it. But when we have the Holy Spirit's presence in our hearts, our lives can follow a completely different and beautiful trajectory out of sin toward righteousness and God. We are no longer bound by sin and guilt. Instead of taking the members of my body—such as my mind, hands, and feet—and using them to steal, lie, hate, abuse, think wrong thoughts, and lust, we can now use them toward virtuous living and present them as "instruments" of righteousness. Everything about ourselves can be used to build instead of destroy, to help others instead of harming others, and to be a testimony to others instead of a disgrace.

Could we do some of that without or before we come to Christ? Sure. But we do not have the same depth of desire, and certainly not the power we receive through the Holy Spirit. That is why the Christian life has been called a supernatural life. Only the Lord and his power can give us the ability to live the life he wants us to live—through making the right choices. What a delightful opportunity for us to choose to live each day in a way we were not freed up to live before our humble decision to use our lives for God's glory.

20. "Sometimes people feel like they have to give God an out."

"Give us this day our daily bread." (Matt. 6:11)

As we were talking in his office, I asked Dr. Robinson, "Why do Christians always say, 'If it be thy will'?" I explained that when I repeated those words in my own prayer life, I felt like I was approaching God with doubts whether he wanted to do, could do, or would do what I was asking. He may have seen the frustration on my face and in my voice because he answered, "I think sometimes people feel like they have to give God an out. If prayer is not answered, they can always say, 'Well, it just wasn't God's will.'"

He then directed me to how Jesus Christ invited his disciples to pray. He explained that Jesus did not ask them to pray, "If it be thy will, give us our daily bread." They were to pray, "Give us our daily bread" (Matt. 6:11).

He used an example about his son Torrey. He explained that if Torrey wanted to go to Six Flags amusement park, he did not want him to say, "Dad, if it be thy will, could we go to Six Flags tomorrow?" Instead, he wanted him to simply say, "Dad, can we go to Six Flags tomorrow?" He explained that even if he responded "No," he wanted Torrey to accept that as the answer from a loving father.

Dr. Robinson also used the example of Paul as he prayed for Epaphroditus. Epaphroditus was a Philippian Christian who assisted Paul in ministry. Paul uses such endearing terms to describe him as "brother," "fellow worker," "fellow soldier," and "your messenger" (Phil. 2:25). The Philippians were distressed when they heard Epaphroditus was sick, probably more ill than they were even aware. Paul informs them that he is "sick almost unto death" (Philippians 2:27). But after Paul prayed for Epaphroditus, God intervened. Dr. Robinson's point was that Paul most likely prayed, "God, please heal Epaphroditus."

He assured me that I too could ask my loving Father for what I wanted without feeling the need to attach "if it be thy will" to each request. There may be times when we are a bit confused what God's will in a particular matter is such as a change of job, opportunity to relocate or purchase of a new home or vehicle. Praying "if it be thy will" is most appropriate knowing he will fulfill our requests in the way he deems best. Dr. Robinson's counsel was that when we earnestly desire something and feel it is in accordance with his will, we should just ask. If the Lord does not answer in the way we desire, we must recognize that he knows what is best. But we ought not to feel obliged to attach "if it be thy will" as a means to explain why our prayers were not answered. God never needs us to provide an excuse for him or defend his actions or inaction.

Want to attach "if it be thy will" to your request? Go ahead. Be careful not to give God an out, though. He needs none. Just ask.

21. "We remember what God forgets, and we forget what God remembers."

"For I will be merciful to their unrighteousness, and their sins and their lawless deeds I will remember no more." (Heb. 8:12)

"And behold, I am coming quickly, and My reward is with Me, to give to every one according to his work." (Rev. 22:12)

One way Dr. Robinson impacted me with God's grace was by helping me understand the intense contrast between God and humanity. What we remember and forget is one area where that difference is so noticeable. We relish the opportunities of reminding others when they have failed us. Years later, the wrong done against us still features prominently in our minds. We forget the good they have done even if it outshines their failures.

God is the opposite. The writer of Hebrews reminds us that God has made a covenant with us: that when we put our trust in Christ, God not only forgives our sins, he forgets them. What a thrill to know that if our failures are not on his mind, they don't have to be on ours either. Along with that, the last chapter of the Bible tells us that he will *not* forget the good that we have done and will abundantly reward us.

I once saw Dr. Robinson verbally mistreated by a colleague of his. I could tell it hurt him deeply. Later, though, I was impressed when he chose not to mention that person's deed against him, and instead the good he had done toward him. At one point, I received a similar verbal abuse from a good friend whose words wounded me to the point that I wept. Afterward, he apologized and asked for my forgiveness. But before he did, I had a decision to make, just like you do: what are we going to remember? What are we going to forget? I decided that whatever God remembered, I needed to remember, and whatever God forgot, I needed to forget.

Similarly, I have a friend who profoundly regrets being responsible for an abortion of a person whose pregnancy he caused. He is now a committed believer who serves the Lord however and whenever he can. He has told me numerous times, "I had to first realize God has forgiven me. Then I had to forgive myself. The second was the hardest." What enabled him to forgive himself was recognizing that because of his repentance, God has forgotten his wrongs and only remembers the good.

As I read the Bible passages again and heard Dr. Robinson's reminder, I was driven to be more Christlike. With God's help, we can discipline our minds to focus on the same things he focuses on. If the Lord does not remember our sins, then what right do we have to remember our neighbors'? If he delights in remembering all the good things we have done, why should we not delight in remembering the good deeds of others?

22. "If a man fails to walk with God, he walks on the edge of an abyss."

Brethren, if anyone among you wanders from the truth, and someone turns him back, let him know that he who turns a sinner from the error of his way will save a soul from death and cover a multitude of sins. (James 5:19–20)

Dr. Robinson had a way of saying things that captured your attention and in a way that stressed the severity of his words. He used to say, "Communication is saying the same thing in different words. You are not likely to tell people something they have not heard, but you can tell it in a way they have never heard it before."

The straightforwardness of this statement of his is an excellent representation of his thoughts on sin. While Dr. Robinson knew the beauty of the grace of God, he never took grace or God's forgiveness lightly. When he spoke of a sin another had committed, he always recognized his capability to commit that same sin himself. I appreciated how he used that knowledge to renew his desire to walk closely with God. He recognized that if a person did not walk with God, each step toward sin would distance the person from the Lord. While we could never lose our eternal salvation, the "abyss" we could face is God's justice and discipline. As a result of this, we should never take lightly what it means to walk away from God.

The Epistle of James is written to believers experiencing great trials after being separated from their loved ones and losing their possessions during a time of persecution. In these final verses, James recognizes that when people go through trials, they can very easily wander from their faith. He encourages them that if someone sees a believer headed in the wrong direction and turns them back toward Christ, he may save them from the judgment of sin God could have brought upon them. That person saved them from what Dr. Robinson called an "abyss" of pain, loneliness, or loss of fellowship with God.

One of the most meaningful sermons I have ever heard a pastor preach was taken from the story of Manasseh in the Old Testament. The pastor's "big idea" was unforgettable: There is no sin so small that God can overlook, but there is no sin so big that God cannot forgive (2 Kings 21:1–18; 2 Chron. 33:10–17). The sermon recognized that every believer sins daily, whether it's through unkind actions, wrong thoughts, selfishness, you name it. What God ultimately wants, though, is for us to call out sin for what it is and to ask for his for his forgiveness. He assures us, "If we confess our sins, He is faithful and just to forgive us our sins and to cleanse us from all unrighteousness" (1 John 1:9).

What Dr. Robinson was addressing here is persistent rebellion: when we know that what we are doing is wrong and yet persist in doing it. As he stated, doing that is like walking on the edge of an abyss: for a while you might get away with it, but the reality is that your actions could easy result in broken relationships, addictive behavior, legal consequences, loss of trust, and even a loss of health. What breaks my heart, and what Dr. Robinson so emphatically highlighted, is that all of those consequences could be prevented if we took sin more seriously.

The time to stop wrongdoing is now, before we fall deeper into sin's darkness. As we confess our sin, we experience the joy that comes with knowing we are forgiven and are back on track in terms of our fellowship with him. We can also rest knowing that in the same way a father disciplines a beloved son (Heb. 12:7), our heavenly Father will do anything he needs to get our attention and draw us back into fellowship with him. While this may come in the form of discipline, everything that God does is in the hope that we will stop drifting away and instead draw close to him.

23. "If you say, 'I would never fall into immorality; that is not my problem,' you will probably be the first to fall."

Brethren, if a man is overtaken in any trespass, you who are spiritual restore such a one in a spirit of gentleness, considering yourself lest you also be tempted. (Gal. 6:1)

At one of the side lectures at Dallas Theological Seminary, Dr. Robinson was addressing the topic of avoiding adultery in the ministry. While I was always intentional with going to all of his lectures, at this particular one I remember thinking, "I want to listen carefully to what he has to say. Fortunately, though, this is something I will never have to worry about. I would never be unfaithful to my wife." Less than ten seconds later, he made the above statement. It impacted me so profoundly that I cannot recall anything else he said from that lecture aside from that sentence.

When I read Galatians 6:1, I realized the biblical basis of what he was saying. When a believer falls into a sin such as adultery, our goal should be to restore, not simply rebuke. One reason that we should respond in such a manner is that we ourselves are not above that temptation. This time we are restoring someone; the next time that someone might need to restore us.

Several years after Dr. Robinson's lecture, a few of my best friends fell into adultery, all within months of each other. At one point, I had just left a weeklong church outreach when a chairman of the board called me to tell me that the pastor had just left town with another man's wife. I remember physically trembling in response to the news, recognizing that what happened to him could very easily happen to me. I was so afraid that I asked my staff if they would pray for me that I would never fall in that area. Gratefully, I can say that I have not been tempted in that way. However, I have never lost the fear that what has happened to others could happen to me.

Let's not deceive ourselves. What has tripped others up could make us stumble as well. We are all vulnerable. The wisest thing we can do is recognize the possibilities and take all the necessary precautions.

24. "No human mind has the ability to fathom what heaven is going to be like."

But as it is written:

> *"Eye has not seen, nor ear heard,*
> *Nor have entered into the heart of man*
> *The things which God has prepared for those*
> *who love Him." (1 Cor. 2:9)*

When you esteem someone as highly as I esteemed Dr. Robinson, you hang on every word they say, whether it was said behind the pulpit or in the midst of a conversation. In the various times I heard him discuss heaven, I could see how much our attempts to comprehend what heaven was going to be like baffled him.

In one of his messages on love, he managed to bring up the subject of heaven. He began by speaking about how the items mentioned in 1 Corinthians 13 will fade away, but love is eternal. As 1 Corinthians 13:7 says, love "bears all things, believes all things, hopes all things, endures all things." Dr. Robinson then honed in on 1 Corinthians 13:12–13: "For now we see in a mirror dimly, but then face to face. Now I know in part, but then I shall know just as I also am known. And now abide faith, hope, and love, these three; but the greatest of these is love." The verses' explication of the eternal nature of love is what led him into the subject of heaven. He made the point that since heaven is grounded in God's eternal love, there is no way for us to know what it is going to be like until we see Christ face to face. As an application, he alluded to 1 Corinthians 2:9, saying that apart from the working of the Holy Spirit no one can understand the deep things of God. "Nor have entered into the heart of man" is one of the strongest ways God could have ever have said that, in terms of spiritual things, what he has prepared for us is beyond our comprehension. As 1 Corinthians 13:12 says, we see things only "dimly." Isaiah 65:17 goes so far as to say that the new heavens and earth will be of such a nature that anything from before then will not be remembered. There is going to be absolutely no resemblance.

I have often wondered why God doesn't tell us more about heaven in the Scriptures. Now I think I know: even if God tried, we would never "get it." Our most grandiose ideas of what heaven will be like don't come close. Obviously, the fact that God himself will be in heaven is what will make it what it is. To be forever in his presence is mind-boggling. Add to that all that an awesome God can create, and heaven becomes utterly mentally unattainable.

As we think of what heaven is going to be like, we ought to "dream on." Think! Imagine! Then, with overflowing excitement, we should realize that we haven't even come close.

PUBLIC SPEAKING AND PREACHING

25. **"Learning how to speak is like learning how to think. If you think clearly, you will speak clearly."**

*Jesus said to him, "You shall love the L*ORD *your God with all your heart, with all your soul, and with all your mind." (Matt. 22:37)*

While I always thought preaching had to do with the way I spoke, Dr. Haddon Robinson emphasized that preaching was more connected with my mind, not just my technical ability to speak well. When it comes down to it, confusing speakers are confused thinkers. Therefore, if I want to speak clearly, then it is essential that I learn how to think clearly.

After hearing these words from Dr. Robinson, I started meditating on Matthew 22:37 because if I love the Lord with my entire mind, I should improve my thinking so my sermons can effectively and clearly communicate biblical truths.

I decided that if I was going to learn to communicate the way Dr. Robinson did, I had to somehow get inside his head and learn how he thought. The first thing I learned was how to *think* about introductions. In other words, how to strike a need, arouse attention, and introduce the text. He also taught me how to *think* about humor: to use humor not for humor's sake, but instead for communication's sake. If an illustration does not demonstrate the point I am making, it has to be thrown out of the message. He trained me to ask myself these questions when approaching the creation of a speech or sermon: What is the text talking about? What is it saying about what it is talking about? Then, as a result of these two questions and their answers, I can determine what I am asking the audience to do. If those two things are not clear in my mind, there is no way I can make them clear in the minds of my audience. If I am confused, my audience will be as well.

While it is important to improve our speaking skills, that development is meaningless if we don't simultaneously improve the way we approach the creation of our message. It is vital to examine our thought process and view it from our audience's perspective. Clarity in the mind produces clarity in the message.

26. "God has not promised to bless your words; he has only promised to bless his."

All Scripture is given by inspiration of God, and is profitable for doctrine, for reproof, for correction, for instruction in righteousness, that the man of God may be complete, thoroughly equipped for every good work. (2 Tim. 3:16–17)

From the use of words such as *doctrine, reproof, correction,* and *instruction* in the above passage, I came to understand what God aims to do in the lives of my listeners through my preaching. He wants to cleanse our lives of what should not be there and replace those things with what should be there. But what does God use to do that? The text says that *Scripture* is inspired by God, and that is what God promises to use as a force of change and personal refinement in our lives. God does not promise to bless a preacher's thoughts, only his own holy, perfect thoughts. As Dr. Robinson described, one who teaches the Scriptures must study them carefully because there is not one passage in the Bible where God promises to use our words.

A message I heard by an evangelist who spoke on 1 Samuel 20:3 made this all "click" in my mind. In that verse, David says to his friend Jonathan, "But truly, as the LORD lives and as your soul lives, there is but a step between me and death." The evangelist then, in a very forceful way, said, "That is what God is saying. There is one step between you and death. You better come to Christ tonight."

At first glance, it would seem like he was preaching God's word. Does the text not say, "There is but one step between me and death"? When I examined the passage, though, I discovered that the passage is not referencing evangelism or coming to Christ. The passage is talking about getting *away* from someone—Jonathan's father who is threatening to kill David. What the verse hinges on is David's warning to Jonathan of the imminent death he could suffer from his father, Saul.

The way the evangelist used that verse was in no way in keeping with God's original intentions. What the passage was actually saying and what the evangelist *said* it was saying were two entirely different things. To ask God to use a human's reconstruction of his own words is a futile exercise. Never has he expressed that we should reorient Scripture for our own needs, and never has he promised to speak through our personal interpretations of the Bible. *Can* God use such a message? Certainly. God can use whatever he wants to use. However, it is his word that has promises attached to it, not ours. It is the Bible that he promises to transform lives with. That's why it is essential that we study a text carefully before centering a sermon on it. We must be certain that we understand its meaning so it is truly the Lord's word we are preaching. If we do that, then we'll know we are speaking the truth and jumping into the passage to dissect it, not exiting from the passage's true meaning by making it say what we want it to say.

In the end, it is a relief to know that God will not bless our faulty, unholy words. He will bless only his own words. Our sanctified task is to repeat them and watch God use them in the way he intended. When accurately rendered by us, his instruments, he will use his word in our preaching and evangelism.

27. "The biggest problem I have had while training preachers has been, strangely enough, getting them to *preach the word*."

Preach the word! Be ready in season and out of season. Convince, rebuke, exhort, with all long-suffering and teaching. (2 Tim. 4:2)

It is a painful thing to watch the suffering of someone who has made such a difference in your life. As I drove to Lancaster, Pennsylvania, in the fall of 2016 for what I knew could be my final time with Dr. Robinson (and it was), it was hard for me to prepare myself for what I was about to face: one of the greatest preachers in America confined to a wheelchair, barely able to whisper.

During my time with him, I felt burdened to ask him a particular question. Forty-three years after he endorsed me and helped develop my gift of evangelism, Bible colleges and seminaries had begun inviting me to come and teach students what he taught me. In preparation for this, I asked him, "In all your years of training preachers how to preach, what is the biggest struggle you have had?" He thought for a second with that characteristic pause of his before whispering the above words.

Why would that be true when Paul's instructions to Timothy and to us are so clear: "Preach the word"? One reason may be lack of know-how. Another may be the perseverance and work it takes to come up with a good sermon. Sometimes, as he explains, the preacher can rattle on about what at first glance the passage *appears* to be saying, not about what it actually is saying. Doing that takes little or no time, preparation, or work. On some occasions, preachers lose focus from the passage and begin focusing on funny anecdotes or unrelated stories—like a recent political headline, a funny thing that happened to their family, or a joke—that they believe highlights the sermon but really just distracts the audience from what the passage is saying.

Dr. Robinson's approach to preaching involved learning how to think, which prepared one to help others learn how to think and invest themselves in unpacking the message. He was known to say, "Thinking is hard work. Thinking about thinking is even harder work." In parallel with the verbs Paul uses in speaking to Timothy, Dr. Robinson highlights the importance of time, study, discipline, and thoughtful effort in preparing a sermon that is truly centered on God's word.

Dr. Robinson's challenge to "preach the word" ought to resonate in everyone's ears as they prepare a sermon. After all, God is not giving us a choice. *Preach the word*!

28. "The stance of a preacher is the stance of a persuader. You are not there to simply teach; you are there to persuade."

And he reasoned in the synagogue every Sabbath, and persuaded both Jews and Greeks. (Acts 18:4)

After my debut as an evangelist, I was fortunate to have kind and complimentary church leaders who not only invited me back but also recommended me to other churches and pastors. To an evangelist who is just getting started, you can imagine what an encouragement that was.

One comment they often made puzzled me, though. Observing how God had just used me to persuade people to come to Christ, they would say, "You are a preacher, but I am a teacher." The idea behind their comment was: "I cannot preach the way you do because I'm a gifted teacher, not a gifted evangelist." I recognize that they were trying to pay me a compliment, but I also feel that they were justifying the lack of enthusiasm and persuasiveness in their own preaching that they saw in mine. They viewed "preachers" as being the only people able to get excited about Scripture and, in the process, excite their congregants to come to Christ or renew their passion for God.

In one of my discussions with Dr. Robinson, I mentioned the pastors' words to him. In his graceful way, he made it clear that what they said was not a biblically justifiable comment. His reasoning was that whenever you stood before an audience, you were not there to simply teach. You were there to persuade people to come to God and focus their lives around him. Dr. Robinson explained that throughout the New Testament the stance of a preacher is the stance of a persuader. What he meant was that God uses you not just to inform your listeners of what God has said, but also to convince them that they ought to act on it now! God wants our obedience, which usually can be spurred on only by an enthusiastic and helpful source.

No verse could better support Dr. Robinson's claim than Acts 18:4. Luke, the author of Acts, characterizes Paul's ministry as being one that not only informs but also convinces. Paul wanted Jews and

Gentiles alike to understand that Jesus Christ was the promised Messiah, as well as enthusiastically trust him to save them from their sins and radically change their lives.

We must have that same goal. People are not saved when they understand the gospel; they are saved only when they receive and apply it. Applying the gospel means seeing yourself as a sinner, recognizing that Jesus Christ was the one who died in your place on the cross and rose again, and trusting him to save you. When we trust Christ as our Savior we have responded with our hearts, not just our heads.

God is responsible for the results of our ministries, but our purpose must be clear. We should ask people to react and do something as a result of our messages, not merely listen. Our aim is to speak in such a way that they see the need to do whatever the Scripture we are speaking from is calling them to do. We need to make their choice to respond to God's word as appealing, exciting, and honest as we possibly can. It's through our nudges that people can be awakened to God's desire for them.

29. "When people come to church on Sunday, they want to know what you can tell them that will help them get through the following week."

Now we exhort you, brethren, warn those who are unruly, comfort the fainthearted, uphold the weak, be patient with all. (1 Thess. 5:14)

Two of the things I admired most about Dr. Robinson was his ability to be such a deep thinker and also so immensely practical in his advice to willing listeners.

In the case of his statement above, he and several other leaders were being informally interviewed. One question they were asked was, "What is one headline you would like to see in the news within the next year?" There were answers such as "peace restored to the Middle East," "poverty eliminated," and "no more terrorism"—which were all good and meaningful. However, Dr. Robinson had the response that may have been the one with which most would identify. He answered, "Cancer cured."

He carried that same practicality into the pulpit. If many pastors were asked, "What is your goal on a Sunday morning?" they may answer, "To preach the word." Dr. Robinson, however, stated that the word was the *means*, not the goal. He stressed that our congregations are sitting before us feeling tired, worried, and lonely; having failed at home or at work; filled with regrets about last week; and a bit afraid of the future. He brought home his idea by asking, "What are you going to say that will get them through the next week?"

The way the Thessalonians ministered to one another is the same way we ought to encourage others from the pulpit. Messages need to be biblical and rooted in the text, but also practical. We cannot address every need on every Sunday; we should speak to the needs that the text we are preaching from addresses.

Though encouragement from the pulpit is vital, it is also important to warn disobedient believers about the consequences of their behavior. In the same way, discouraged believers need comfort and reassurance, and those wondering how they can go on should feel strengthened after an uplifting sermon. That may seem like a lot to achieve in one sermon; however, messages that are extremely biblical and applicable should accomplish all that. As a result of a particularly powerful and relevant sermon, people may leave feeling guilty about the things they have done and asking for God's forgiveness. Others may find just the answer they need to a dilemma they are facing. Another is more hopeful leaving the service than when they came in. Some will leave recognizing that, with patience and endurance, a brighter day will come. Despite all the varying degrees someone can be affected, the beauty of a practical sermon is that in some way every believer leaves feeling helped.

After your congregation leaves on Sunday, remember that they all go back to work on Monday. What have you said that will guide them toward a more God-centered, productive, and self-refining week?

30. "The art of preaching isn't hinged upon knowing what to put into your message, but rather what to take out."

Till I come, give attention to reading, to exhortation, to doctrine. . . . Meditate on these things; give yourself entirely to them, that your progress may be evident to all. Take heed to yourself and to the doctrine. Continue in them, for in doing this you will save both yourself and those who hear you. (1 Tim. 4:13, 15–16)

A preacher who gives himself to being an expositor of the Scriptures faces a tremendous problem: It is not having too little to say; it is having too much. It is on the subject of how to handle that dilemma that Dr. Robinson taught me one of the most valuable lessons in speaking.

From the pulpit, we face those confronted with spiritual battles. Since we are called on to preach the word, we must mediate on whatever passage we are about to use so that we can best help people win those battles. We must think about the meaning and details of the passage, as well as how the sentences relate to one another before we can apply them to our audience. Paul told Timothy what every preacher is to heed: A preacher is to immerse himself in the word so that he is able to explain truth that relates to both a person's salvation and sanctification. A preacher ought to be able to say, "Oh, how I love Your law! It is my meditation all the day" (Ps. 119:97). The gift, but also hindrance, in studying the Bible is that the deeper we dig into any passage, the more we discover. We soon find that we are not eating from a dish; we are dining at a smorgasbord. There is more there than can be said in one message. Covering everything the passage says is virtually impossible.

It is in situations like these when Dr. Robinson's approach to preaching becomes particularly pertinent. By wrapping the message around a single "big idea" that comes straight from the text, we can determine what to put in and what to leave out. We should leave in the explanations, illustrations, and humor essential to communicating the main idea, and the rest we should take out. We can't be concerned about whether the people know everything the passage said. We should focus on saying one thing so strongly and effectively that our listeners will never forget it and will apply our helpful advice enthusiastically and successfully.

The word is jam-packed with spiritual truth, which means that *any* passage contains more than you can say in one message. We are called to speak on eternity, not for eternity. So, let's ask ourselves what is crucial to leave in and what can be taken out. Knowing that is truly the art of preaching.

31. "The passage has to hit you before it hits the audience."

Search me, O God, and know my heart;
Try me, and know my anxieties;
And see if there is any wicked way in me,
And lead me in the way everlasting.
*   (Ps. 139:23–24)*

Dr. Robinson never reduced preaching to an intellectual experience. He was careful to explain that as you studied a passage in preparation to speak on it, the truth of that verse or paragraph had to first impact you, otherwise it would not impact the audience. If it hasn't touched you, it is unlikely it will touch them. He modeled that when he spoke. Whenever I heard him, I could sense God had placed a burden on his heart to speak to us on a particular Bible passage or subject.

One time I heard Dr. Robinson speak on the parable of the good Samaritan. He explained that Jesus was answering the question, "Who is my neighbor?" in Luke 10:25–37. The big idea of his sermon was, "The person who is near and whose need you can meet is your neighbor." He followed that up with a way he personally applies the passage to his life: "I cannot assume if I have enough money for two loaves of bread, that one is for me and one is for the freezer. I have to assume that one is for me and the other may be for a needy neighbor." Because of his vulnerability in explaining how the passage touched him, I was even more arrested by the passage and his sermon.

Another particularly potent sermon I heard was on 1 Corinthians 11:27–34. The pastor's main idea was that your preparation for and how you approach the Communion table will be a deciding factor on how God judges you and could be a matter of life or death. He echoed the warning about partaking in the Lord's Supper without having dealt with known sin in our own lives. The passage reads, "But let a man examine himself, and so let him eat of the bread and drink of the cup" (v. 28). What I found to be the most interesting and convicting was how the pastor revealed what he had to get right with another believer. Following the message, I was amazed to see person after person reconcile with one another after hearing not only the passage but the pastor's personal testimony. That really showed how the passage meant something to him first and then to the audience.

Dr. Robinson explained that God wants to speak through you, but first he wants to speak to you. God does that through his word—the same word you are about to deliver to others. That is why any passage we select for our message needs to resonate with us first. The psalmist reflected that spirit. He wanted God to search him and test him the way a refiner tests metal, so he would not be like the wicked in the previous verses. Since God knew him better than anyone, he wanted God to examine all the things he was anxious about and remove anything offensive. In short, he was saying, "God, speak to me. Change me." God is not just concerned about our audience; he is concerned about *us*. As God convicts us and directs us toward the life we ought to live, he can then use us to convict others how they ought to live.

When we share something that has made a difference in us with our audience, it has a better chance of making an impact because we exude passion for it. With that passion comes the attitude: "This passage changed me. I can't wait to see how it can change you too."

32. "When you say, 'Thus saith the Lord,' you better be right. That is an awesome claim."

Be diligent to present yourself approved to God, a worker who does not need to be ashamed, rightly dividing the word of truth. (2 Tim. 2:15)

There is no question about it: I would have still been an evangelist even had I not gone to Dallas Theological Seminary. My time there did not make me an evangelist; however, I do question if I would have been as good an expositor. Through the input of Dr. Robinson, I became burdened to be utterly faithful to Scripture. That meant I had to confidently do what Paul told Timothy—"rightly divide the word of truth"—and explain the Bible accurately and carefully.

Dr. Robinson eloquently explained to me that this meant I had to first study whatever passage of Scripture I spoke from in its original context. How could I be certain what the Bible was saying to the people of *our* day unless I first understood what it was saying to the people of *that* day? When God spoke, he was speaking to people living in a specific cultural context. Once I understood how they understood the word of God, I could properly apply it to my audience. Dr. Robinson helped me, as well as many others, understand that there was no way to deduce a passage's meaning and apply it to our audiences without first grasping what it meant to the people of that day.

What adds to the critical nature of this task is that I am not presenting the word of Churchill, Augustine, or Shakespeare; I'm claiming to speak on behalf of God. Not a god, but *the* God. To in any way misrepresent what he said and why he said it would be both irresponsible and wrong. In a proper sense, I had to know the "fear of God" when handling the Scriptures. I am not preaching in a way to say, "This is what I think." I am stating as an expositor, "This is what God says."

The place where Dr. Robinson's advice became meaningful and understandable was when one of my preaching classes met in his home in Dallas. I remember it as though it were yesterday. As we sat in a circle in his living room, he put his stocking feet up on the coffee table and began to explain how he processed the book of James. Who was James writing to? Who are these "twelve tribes which are scattered abroad"? Why does James say, "Count it all joy when you fall into various trials"? What trials, and how could a person possibly do that? Nobody enjoys hardship! Why ask God for wisdom? Wisdom about what? What is James's point in using the example of a poor and rich brother in chapter one? Chapter by chapter, Dr. Robinson explained the questions we had to wrestle with and answer if we were to explain it to an audience. In this firm example, he solidified the truth that only through such careful study could we then be certain that "thus saith the Lord."

I left those times in Dr. Robinson's home understanding how to study God's word, apply it, and preach it like I never knew before. I now could "rightly divide the word" and properly preach it to others. In order for all of us to apply that idea, we must constantly remind ourselves that speaking on behalf of God can never be taken lightly. We must be sure we are right about our interpretations. People are leaving our sermons or speeches with the understanding that they have heard from God. We had better be certain that they have.

33. "The problem is that too many preachers tear the passage apart in their studies and then don't put it back together before they step into the pulpit."

"And I will give you shepherds according to My heart, who will feed you with knowledge and understanding." (Jer. 3:15)

To explain what a passage of the Bible says, you have to know what it means. Hours of study must be spent tearing the passage apart, examining it in its context, and defining the main words. God's thoughts have reason and flow to them.

Dr. Robinson explained that tearing the passage apart was where a lot of preachers stop. They then take all that exegesis into the pulpit. What they forgot to do was put the passage back together again. What he meant by that is that they tear the passage completely apart in their study, look at the meaning of the major nouns and verbs—their word studies are often extensive—and observe how phrases are related to each other, and then they try to put themselves in the shoes of the audience the passage is speaking to.

If a particular city is mentioned, they want to know why. If particular person is addressed, they want to know as much as possible about him or her. Was this a morning or afternoon event? What else may be occurring that the passage does not address? What is the mood of the passage—somber, expectant, excited? By the time they are done, they have a grip on just about everything happening in the passage. The problem is they take all those details and findings with them into the pulpit. They try to not leave out anything they have learned. As a result, the audience doesn't understand what ties all that together and how the passage applies to them. After hearing a confusing sermon, weeks later they most likely could not tell you what the preacher said. All they could tell you was that he said *a lot*. As Dr. Robinson so eloquently stated, the preacher tore the passage apart, but he did not put it together again in a way their congregation could understand or apply to their lives.

When I reflect on his observation, I think of God's words through Jeremiah. What makes them pertinent is that throughout Scripture God provides shepherds for his people to teach them to be faithful, devoted leaders who impart truth. Church leaders provide that same guidance through the preaching of the word. Just as God gives the leaders knowledge and understanding, pastors and preachers are to impart the same to their congregations. Our need is to not merely feed people with bits of truth, but to show them how God's thoughts go together. As the passage in Jeremiah states, we want them to not only know but also *understand*. The Lord has reasons and purposes behind everything he says. As Dr. Robinson taught, the central truth of the passage carefully tied together and supported from the text helps people more than disjointed thoughts and ideas.

Anyone can tear the passage apart. But only skilled communicators can put it back together again in a way that will connect with their listeners. We are not behind the pulpit to overwhelm people with the definition of each Greek or Hebrew word or our knowledge and intelligence. We are there to impart God's knowledge and understanding. And that is why God has us in the pulpit—not simply to talk but to communicate his truth.

LEADERSHIP

34. "We have led you. Now it's time for you to lead us."

And the things that you have heard from me among many witnesses, commit these to faithful men who will be able to teach others also. (2 Tim. 2:2)

One evening, after our board meeting for Evan-Tell had ended, I drove Dr. Robinson to his daughter Vicki's house to spend the remainder of the weekend with her. As we were sitting in my car outside of her house, I began using the time to seek his advice about life and ministry matters.

Suddenly, he looked at me and said, "I need to talk to you about something." I had no idea what he had in mind. When Dr. Robinson wanted to talk to you about something, you listened! I asked, with probably a bit of trembling and not having any idea what he had in mind, "What's that?" He replied, "We have led you. Now it's time for you to lead us." He then explained that as EvanTell got started, the board of directors had to lead me. Inexperienced as I was, there were only a few areas where they had to tell me what to do. As a result of my preparation and hard work, Dr. Robinson explained that it was now time for me to lead them.

I realized that what Dr. Robinson was doing was freeing me up to take control and guide the company.

In doing so, he was following Paul's admonition to Timothy to commit what he knew to me so that one day I could teach others what he taught me. To do that, though, I had to be freed up to take charge and move out from under his constant supervision. That was a turning point in my life and leadership. I began by laying out a three-year plan for EvanTell, asking my colleagues for their help and support. I told them about areas in which we had to take a risk, like all leaders have to, and asked them to take that risk with me. When it was time to completely restructure the ministry due to growth, I explained to them why such a restructuring was essential.

After having been a leader for some time now, I have seen those who cannot give up that kind of leadership when they have been in it for so long. I can understand why: it is extremely difficult to trust anyone to take good care of your company or ministry when you know it so thoroughly inside and out. I know of a CEO of a nonprofit who decided to give up the leadership of the ministry to a person he had personally mentored, but only when he was out of town. When he returned to the office, he took back the reins, causing disunity within the staff and harm to the ministry's outreach.

That faith and trust in others' abilities to lead is what made Dr. Robinson such a good leader himself. He recognized others' gifts and instead of questioning their skills, he humbled himself and allowed them to lead where they were most adept. At the cost of his own leadership, he encouraged the growth and flourishing of others' talents in the hopes that they could be a better leader than him in that particular area.

Are you freeing people up to lead? If so, are you letting them lead you?

35. "As a minister, you will have your ministry either blasted or blessed by your spouse."

Two are better than one,
Because they have a good reward for their labor.
For if they fall, one will lift up his companion.
But woe to him who is alone when he falls,
For he has no one to help him up. (Eccl. 4:9–10)

During another one of those informal times with Dr. Robinson just after class, several of us had gathered around him to discuss marriage. He spoke transparently about the help that his wife, Bonnie, had been to him. Since he was interacting with future preachers—many of whom were not yet married—he wanted us to know what a serious decision we would be making if we chose to get married.

What made his words so meaningful was getting to know Bonnie and seeing how they interacted together. It wasn't hard for me to see that Bonnie's two biggest priorities were the Lord and her husband, in that order. She was immensely devoted to the Savior and would do anything he wanted of her. If her husband had to be away speaking, come home, and head right to the seminary, I could tell that he had her firm support. When we met for class in their home in Dallas, she greeted us as we walked in the door. If refreshments were offered, she served them. When I got my Doctor of Ministry degree from Gordon-Conwell, he wanted the class to have an informal time with him and Bonnie. I soon learned how admired she was because she made it a point to minister to the women on campus, encourage them, and be available to them. She personally told me how much she enjoyed being there for them. Also, whenever Dr. Robinson needed transportation, whether it was to the airport or wherever he needed to be, she was there to assist. There were times Dr. Robinson mentioned how interacting with Bonnie helped him develop thoughts he had. I am absolutely convinced that only eternity will reveal the full impact Bonnie had on Dr. Robinson's ministry throughout their entire sixty-six years of marriage.

Dr. Robinson made it clear that a spouse who was not behind you could destroy your whole ministry, whether you're a pastor, missionary, youth or music director, Christian education director, or small group leader. At the time of that conversation with Dr. Robinson, I was one of the unmarrieds but seriously dating Tammy, who later became my wife. His words caused us to have some long talks about my desire to go into full-time evangelism, since giving up that dream wasn't an option for me. I was thrilled to find out that she was as excited as I was, and I'm blessed to say that her position has never changed.

Ecclesiastes speaks to the benefits of the right kind of companion: one who is there to lift you up when you fall. No one is more blessed when that kind of companion is his or her spouse. After all, nothing is of more value than a spouse who gives encouragement and wise counsel as it is needed, assures their partner that they will support them wherever and however they can, seeks ways to lighten the load, assists them in every way imaginable in raising children who desire to walk in the footsteps of Christ, and prays fervently for them. They are there 24/7. The two of them are a team; they push each other forward, not backward.

Although certainly true of ministers, Dr. Robinson's words would fit any profession. The companion needed is one of whom the commendation is made, "We would not have accomplished what we did without our spouses." The one we marry will impact how far we go in our profession, and how thoroughly we are able to pursue our dreams.

36. "If I were a pastor of a church, I would ordain people to the workplace."

Then the LORD spoke to Moses, saying: "See, I have called by name Bezalel the son of Uri, the son of Hur, of the tribe of Judah. And I have filled him with the Spirit of God, in wisdom, in understanding, in knowledge, and in all manner of workmanship."
(Exod. 31:1–3)

Many years ago, when I wanted to get my Doctor of Ministry degree, all I knew was that I wanted it to be from a different part of the country from where I had received my master's degree and that I wanted it to be in a field that would stretch me. My confusion and uncertainty once again offered me the perfect opportunity to call on the wise advice of my friend and mentor, Dr. Robinson.

He explained that he was teaching a Doctor of Ministry course centered on Christianity in the workplace at Gordon-Conwell Theological Seminary in Massachusetts. They were putting nine CEOs of for-profit companies alongside nine CEOs of nonprofit companies. He said, "I would love to have you in the course." Decision made! Case closed!

The class focused on the fact that every Christian committed to the Lord was in full-time ministry, whether they served an as engineer, contractor, dentist, or hair stylist. A person's work was to be their worship as well as their mission field. To elucidate, there is the example of the two kinds of people who work. One says, "I am an engineer who happens to be a Christian." The other says, "I am a Christian called to serve God as an engineer." The first sees what he does as a job; the second sees what he does as his mission field. God wants the latter mind-set. Having a combination of CEOs from for- and nonprofit companies was valuable because, in our class, the majority of the CEOs of nonprofits gave ideas from a ministry perspective, while the CEOs of for-profit companies explained what was and was not permissible in a secular workplace. Dr. Robinson was not just a professor but a great facilitator, because he knew how to draw out our ideas on everything from leadership styles, character issues, supervising employees, discipline issues, to crisis management. The purpose was to understand how those topics affect one's opportunities for spiritual discussions inside and outside the workplace as well as one's own faith.

When Dr. Robinson made the above comment, many echoed an audible "yes." All of us had seen people who wanted to be a strong witness for Christ in the workplace not be regarded with the same amount of potential impact and importance as full-time clergy. The fact is that some committed Christians have more opportunities to witness to unbelievers than members of the clergy do, and they are more zealous when those opportunities arise.

Bezalel is a superb example of someone in full-time ministry in the workplace. He was a workplace leader, not a preacher, yet he was filled with the Spirit of God. Because his God-given ability was to work with precious metals, masonry, and woodwork, God chose him to be the principal designer and chief builder of the holy tabernacle. The phrase "I have been called" conveys the idea that he was designated and appointed by God to superintend the work. Bezalel was absolutely in full-time ministry, just not in a traditional way.

Dr. Robinson's point was that if we ordain people to the mission field, which many churches do, why not ordain Christians to their workplaces? Those too are mission fields. We should serve God enthusiastically everywhere we work. We don't need to be pastors in order for our workplaces to be mission fields. Congratulations! We are in all in full-time ministry.

37. "The good thing is you don't know what you don't know."

Whoever loves instruction loves knowledge,
But he who hates correction is stupid. (Prov. 12:1)

At the time of Dr. Robinson's comment, EvanTell had been in existence for about two years, and I knew Dr. Robinson well enough by then to be aware that he meant this as an encouraging comment. However, I struggled in understanding what he meant. It wasn't until I started studying books on leadership that I began to understand his meaning.

In those books, I discovered that a leader typically goes through four stages: (1) I don't know what I don't know, (2) I now know what I need to learn, (3) I have learned what I didn't know, and (4) I am now living out and teaching others what I have learned. All Dr. Robinson was saying was that at the first stage I had no idea what I had to learn because I did not even have a grasp on what I needed to know. After discovering this, I felt immediate relief. I do not have to criticize myself because part of growing as a leader is listening and learning. I just have to read, interact with other leaders, and do everything in my power to learn what I don't know.

That is why the encouragement and warning of Proverbs 12:1 becomes so meaningful. A love for instruction and learning has a tremendous reward: wisdom to skillfully live our lives as we receive needed discipline and correction. Our lives are enhanced as we learn what we didn't even realize we needed to know.

What happens to the person who hates such instruction? Proverbs minces no words. The verse calls that person "stupid." The word literally means dull minded, as animals are. That person learns nothing. Wherever they are in their skill level is where they remain. What they do five years from now is no better or sharper than where they are now. Know-how has not been enhanced.

On the other hand, if we give ourselves to learning, we become better at what we do. Our awareness of and openness to internal changes shows itself in the quality of our work and even allows us to mentor others and give them our knowledge. More doors of opportunity open to us as people see how good we have become at what we do. Regardless of the profession, people often say of such a person, "They are one of our most skilled workers."

Understand that instruction deals with both character and conduct. Proverbs emphasizes not just developing our abilities, but also growing and maturing as a person. That growth impacts what we do, how we do it, and how we relate to others as we do it.

As EvanTell grew in age, I soon learned all the things that Dr. Robinson had in mind. There was a host of things as a young leader I had to learn: developing a three- or five-year plan, hiring people who knew more than I do, what to delegate and what not to, how to effectively supervise a multi-person staff, developing what would eventually be a governance board of directors, how to get proper return on our investment, developing our ministry's core values, managing conflict within a team, and numerous other items. While at the time I did not know all these important elements to lead a company, to learn them was challenging and rewarding in the best of ways.

As leaders, we should not merely receive instruction, we should love it. Loving it has to do with attitudes, and attitudes will then affect actions. We will not learn unless we have a heart to learn.

Dr. Robinson's point, demonstrated through both his words and his very demeanor, was that there was no need for me to apologize for what I didn't know. Every leader starts there. I just had to set myself on a track to learn. Imagine the satisfaction we'll feel in looking back and seeing how much we have learned and grown, and the fulfillment in being able to help others along their own journeys.

38. "We have enough books on how to be a good leader. I think we need more on how to be a good follower."

Likewise you younger people, submit yourselves to your elders. Yes, all of you be submissive to one another, and be clothed with humility, for

> *"God resists the proud,*
> *But gives grace to the humble." (1 Pet. 5:5)*

One time as we were discussing a book in the Doctor of Ministry course that we were given to read and write a report on, Dr. Robinson paused. It was one of those pauses that signaled he was thinking deeply about what he was about to say. Then he made the above remark. He elaborated it by explaining that as a result of our emphasis on the importance of good leadership, we have overlooked the importance of good followers. Good leaders need good followers who respect the direction they are headed, support them in any way they can, and help them achieve their goals.

Good followers, he pointed out, will help leaders succeed beyond what even they thought they could do. That is one reason he once said in the context of the church, "Great preachers do not produce great churches. Instead, great churches produce great preachers." If the people of the church are the support they ought to be, then the preacher ends up becoming one of the greatest preachers he could be.

Peter talks about the importance of people being proper leaders in the body of Christ through example and exhortation (1 Pet. 5:1–4). He explains the importance of leaders being servant minded—serving not because they have to but because, as people of integrity who desire to shepherd people toward their best lives, they want to show people how to live instead of merely telling them. In support of Dr. Robinson's observation, Peter does not stop there. He stresses the importance of good followers. While he is speaking in the context of the church, it still holds true that all leaders cannot effectively lead if they do not have people who are willing to submit to the leader's will. To submit means a willingness to put oneself under the authority of another. It is interesting that he mentions submitting not only to the elders but also to "one another." The body of Christ is such that we all may be called to lead and follow at one time or another. For a period, I may be called to lead so you must follow, and but at another time you may be called to lead so I must follow. The essential ingredient to this swap? Humility!

The summer between my final year of undergraduate school and my first year of seminary, I took an interim pastorate position in Baltimore, Maryland. I was going to be their pastor for three months before I went back to school. I took the opportunity because, although I knew I was going into full-time evangelism, I wanted to experience being a pastor. On my first Sunday, someone said to me, "Did anyone tell you that we had a split last Sunday?" That question stopped me in my tracks. Here I was having just completed college with virtually no experience. I needed God's help—and fast. As I walked up to the pulpit, God put these words on my heart: "I understand you had a split last Sunday. All I ask is that we don't talk about it. It is in the past. Let's move forward together." Thankfully, we had a great summer: attendance climbed, unbelievers came to Christ, and believers were strengthened in their Christian walk. I was willing to lead, but what truly made the difference were the people willing to follow my leadership. In fact, I blossomed as a leader that summer because of the congregation's expression of confidence in me.

A church I spoke at in Michigan regularly coordinated "Friendship Dinners" at a restaurant to reach non-Christians. For this outreach, the pastor—who was a good leader whom people willingly followed—decided to ask a woman in his congregation to lead. While normally she followed his leadership, in working through the details of the outreach, he put himself under her leadership: a clear example of being "submissive to one another." It was an effective outreach that allowed numerous people to come to Christ.

The above scenario begs the questions: How good of a follower are you? Do you make it easier or harder for leaders to lead? Is your attitude and demeanor such that if someone else was the leader, they would want you on their team?

39. "I know that is what I suggested; that was a bad decision."

Behold, I was brought forth in iniquity,
And in sin my mother conceived me.
Behold, You desire truth in the inward parts,
And in the hidden part You will make
me to know wisdom. (Ps. 51:5–6)

At one meeting of the board of directors of EvanTell, Dr. Robinson introduced an idea for what we could do with our end-of-the-year funds. Several years later, the results we desired were not achieved, causing me to question whether we should continue the policy. I shared this with Dr. Robinson as we prepared for our next board meeting, and he listened and agreed. To make sure that he did not want to continue the policy and to respect his wishes if there was something I overlooked, I reminded him that he was the one who had introduced the idea. He acknowledged this and admitted that, in retrospect, it was a bad decision.

I do not think he knew understood how much he taught me about leadership that day. His words expressed to me the idea that leaders don't always have to be right. They just have to have the character and integrity to admit bad choices. Looking back, I can see why his example was so effective. I had wrongly assumed that leaders who make wrong decisions were bad leaders. However, that is a very unhealthy approach to leadership and can even hold us back from taking risks because we are fearful of not succeeding.

Dr. Robinson once shared a story about when he was harshly accused of putting into action a bad procedure in fund-raising. The person was totally off base, not even knowing what was done, and Dr. Robinson pointed that out to him. To his credit, the man acknowledged his hasty judgment and asked for Dr. Robinson's forgiveness. At the same time, Dr. Robinson felt like his own response to the man could have been better and asked him for his forgiveness as well. Through the story, Dr. Robinson was an example of how leaders are not perfect. They do and will make mistakes and wrong decisions.

Years ago, EvanTell developed a program that was used to train thousands in personal evangelism. It cost us a great deal of money. I made the mistake, though, of covering those costs with a loan instead of getting the project underwritten. That debt hung over us for years until we paid it off. Looking back, the idea of the training program was right, but my decision of how to finance it was wrong. Did I ever learn! Thanks to Dr. Robinson, my views on mistakes are so much healthier. Now when I blunder, I love to say to people, "Please forgive me. That is the first mistake I made since the last five."

Psalm 51:6 is too seldom applied to leadership. From the day he was born, David acknowledged that he was not without sin. Translated into leadership, that means there will be times we make wrong decisions. At best, we are flawed people. Our judgments about what to do will not always be the best. In no way is every wrong decision a sinful one, but our poor choices prove that we are depraved people. We are born as sinners, not as perfect people. Truthfulness about bad decisions and wisdom to make better ones transform us into stronger leaders.

EVANGELISM

40. "The way you feel about the worst sin in your mind is the way God feels about sin in general."

"For out of the heart proceed evil thoughts, murders, adulteries, fornications, thefts, false witnesses, blasphemies. These are the things which defile a man, but to eat with unwashed hands does not defile a man." (Matt. 15:19–20)

Every one of us have sins we deem worse than others, usually a result from a painful experience that highlighted the horrors of that particular sin. Murder is horrible in everyone's mind, but to me it is especially hideous. As a hunter, I recognize that the harvesting of one's first buck is a big deal and should never be forgotten. I was twenty-one when a buck in the mountains of Pennsylvania ran past me, paused, and afforded me the shot I needed. To say I was excited would be an understatement. After my hunting day was over, I couldn't wait to show off my first buck, so I sat by the truck and waited until my fellow hunters returned at the end of the day. Ray, one of the hunters in our group, also scored that day not long after I did, and so the two of us reveled in telling and retelling our experiences. The day is as vivid in my mind as though it happened yesterday. Our shared experiences bonded us as fellow hunters into good friends.

You can imagine my dismay when about a year later my sister called to tell me that Ray had been murdered. He went to the apartment complex he owned to collect rent and two men asked him to step inside as they wrote out a check. Once inside, they stabbed him multiple times, stuck his body in a garbage bag, and then dumped it by a country road. When my sister gave me the news, I was horrified. All I could think was, "No, not Ray! Not my hunting buddy." To this day, whenever I read or hear of a murder, Ray comes to mind. All sin is serious but because of my personal experience with the murder of a friend, it tops the list.

When Dr. Robinson made the above comment, it spoke to my heart. When he spoke of thievery, murder, a person who left his or her mate for another person, or someone filled with hate and revenge, it always seemed to strike him how easily he too could commit those sins. They were sinners, but so was he. As I studied the above passage I was struck by a simple fact: Jesus Christ confronted the scribes and Pharisees and all their traditions by pointing out that the heart, not the hands or the mind, is the source of sin.

With that knowledge, Dr. Robinson's words take on much deeper meaning. In God's eyes, all sin that results from a corrupted heart is hideous, including the sin I treat so lightly such as unkind words or selfish attitudes. The way I feel about murder is the same way God feels about my impatience or rudeness.

As a result, we should look at our sins with just as much disdain as we look at others'. Doing so will deepen our appreciation for grace. Yes, others need grace and forgiveness, but so do we. This knowledge also has the capability to increase our love for sinners everywhere. God loves us with all our sinfulness, so we can love others with theirs. The nature of their sin is not the issue. It is the fact that they are sinners just like us.

If we think the sins of others are so repulsive, we are right. But we must pause right there and remind ourselves of our own sin. When we do that, we will end up thanking God that his grace is wide enough to include all of us.

41. "If you start with the presupposition that the ways of God have to be understood by men, limited atonement makes more sense than unlimited atonement. The problem is that you started with a faulty presupposition."

For there is one God and one Mediator between God and men, the Man Christ Jesus, who gave Himself a ransom for all, to be testified in due time. (1 Tim. 2:5–6)

Dr. Robinson had a way of taking discussions about theological issues and wrapping them up in a rather succinct way. Today, as well as all through my years in seminary, there have been discussions about whom Christ died for. Did he die for those whom he knew would come to him (a view called "limited atonement") or did he die for everyone, everywhere (a view called "unlimited atonement")?

The above Scriptures are clear: he died for all. "Ransom" refers to the price that was paid for our sins when Jesus Christ, our mediator, died in our place and paid for our sin in full. Those who say that he died only for those who would trust him as Savior explain that the word *all* there refers to all *believers*. The problem is the text does not say "all believers"; it says "all."

Dr. Robinson explained why some prefer to say that Jesus died only for those who would trust him. To those who believe Christ died only for Christians, it seems like Christ's death would be wasted on those who don't believe because they will not receive his substitutionary death on their behalf. Dr. Robinson admitted that to the human mind, this viewpoint does make logical sense. However, more importantly he recognized that the ways of God do not have to be understandable to human minds. We all should take God at his word, accept Scripture for what it says, and leave the rest to God.

This conclusion ought to give us an excitement to approach anyone and say, "Christ died for you." After all, that *is* what the text says, and if it makes sense to God, then it does not have to be understandable to me.

42. "The message behind the gospel is this: Be satisfied with the thing that satisfied God."

And He Himself is the propitiation for our sins, and not for ours only but also for the whole world. (1 John 2:2)

Because of my heart for evangelism, nothing Dr. Robinson said meant more to me than when he spoke of the gospel and evangelism. From the very start of my time at Dallas, I heard him express concern for people who focus on the wrong thing and miss the real message of the gospel.

There are many unique elements tied to traditional evangelism and the ways people are invited to come to Christ. Some typical responses to evangelism include walking down an aisle to the front of a church to talk with a pastor or deacon, raising a hand while everyone's eyes are closed during an evangelistic prayer, passing in a signed card with a profession of faith, or meeting with a counselor to discuss how one becomes a Christian. All of this is beautiful and helpful when used properly, but it is important we don't muddy the water and distract them from the message to which the people are being asked to respond. It is not an aisle, a raised hand, a card, or a room we meet in that accomplishes our right standing before God.

When Dr. Robinson made the above comment, I had never heard the meaning behind Jesus' death and resurrection expressed any better. God was not asking me to walk an aisle, raise my hand, or sign a card to declare my faith in him. Those might be how I demonstrate my interest in becoming a Christian and, when used properly, can be useful. But what God asks us to do is acknowledge and accept the only thing that satisfied his righteous anger against sin: the death of his Son.

Propitiation means satisfaction. Because our holy God cannot tolerate sin, he punished his perfect Son where he should have punished us. Jesus Christ took our place and died as our substitute. Then, on the third day, he rose again, proving his victory over sin and death. The wrath of God against sin was satisfied in his Son's sacrifice. Therefore, we have to come to God as a sinner, recognize that Christ died in our place and rose again, and place our trust in Christ alone to save us. As Jesus promised: "Most assuredly, I say to you, he who believes in Me has everlasting life" (John 6:47).

Dr. Robinson's point was that what satisfied God was the death of his Son and that *alone* makes us acceptable in his sight. People can try to get to heaven through good deeds or other misguided paths, but we must remind ourselves that what satisfied the Lord has to be the only thing that satisfies us: Christ's sacrifice. Our trust must be in Christ alone as our basis for a right standing with God. That's why we do not have to concern ourselves with not being good enough to be accepted by God. We never will be! That's also why we will never be too sinful for him to save. His death satisfied the wrath of God against *all* sin.

When we trust in him and him alone to receive eternal life, we are "satisfied with the thing that satisfied God." In terms of our eternal justification before God, he is all we have.

43. "Everyone you meet is going to live forever; the only question is where. What are you doing to make the difference?"

"He who believes in the Son has everlasting life; and he who does not believe the Son shall not see life, but the wrath of God abides on him." (John 3:36)

People follow their leaders, congregations follow their pastors, and students follow their professors. In many things, they are more apt to do what the leaders do than what their leaders say. That means in evangelism that if the leaders talk about the lost, followers talk about the lost. If the leaders talk *to* the lost, followers talk to the lost. Interacting with Dr. Robinson was so energizing, because it was in his company that I truly felt my gift of evangelism grow and thrive. I had wanted to talk to the lost already, but even more so as I spent time with him.

I think one reason Dr. Robinson had such a concern for the lost was his mature and eternal perspective on life. He often meditated on what is important in life and what isn't. Material possessions don't matter. They will go up in smoke. It's people who truly matter. As a result, probably nothing he shared with me have I repeated more than his above statement. He did not just say it, though; he believed it. That is why he would talk to the lost.

One of my favorite stories he told me was when he conversed with a man who quite bluntly told him that he had no concern for "that stuff." With a spirit of truth and grace, Dr. Robinson asked him how much time he had spent seriously considering the claims of Christ. The man admitted that he had not given those claims thought or evaluation. Dr. Robinson encouraged him to do so and reminded him, "I have a lot more respect for the person who thinks it through and rejects it than the one who doesn't take the time to give them serious consideration." That comment pierced the man to the extent that he agreed to at least consider who Christ claimed to be.

I did weeklong outreaches for twenty years and saw many come to Christ. After all those years, I noticed that it is harder to get people to church and out during the week. I think this could be because the message never changes, but the method does. I knew Dr. Robinson often spoke at "Friendship Dinners"—a gathering Christians invite their non-Christian friends to attend. People knew that the evening and dinner was spiritual in nature. After some songs, a testimony, and dinner, a message was given. To switch things up, I decided to do "Friendship Dinners" and loved them because often just under half of the audience was unbelievers. It was Dr. Robinson's experience and advice that so helped me develop that outreach as well as EvanTell.

Some people are open to change right now, and you can make an immediate difference in their lives through evangelizing. Help your church sponsor an evangelistic outreach. Invite a non-Christian friend of yours to an outreach event. Invite non-Christian neighbors over for dinner with the hope of sharing the gospel with them in your home. Reach out to a neighbor in need. Helping them with a physical need may allow you both to grow a friendship and eventually encounter the opportunity to discuss spirituality. Invite a coworker to watch the Super Bowl with you. Contact now may open up conversations later. Ask a coworker to go to lunch with you and seek to engage in a thoughtful, gentle spiritual discussion. Do business with non-Christians. Write a letter to a lost relative telling them what they mean to you and clearly explain the gospel. Thank a grocery store clerk for her friendly service, give her an attractive tract that clearly explains the gospel, and invite her to call you with any questions. The possibilities are almost endless. The more non-Christians you know, the more opportunities there are. You can make a difference in anyone's life right now.

Because of Dr. Robinson, I now look at everyone I meet as "forever" people. Whether they will be in heaven or in hell, they will be there forever. John 3:36 uses the present tense. At this very moment people either already have eternal life and will be forever in his presence, or the wrath of God abides on them. If nothing changes, they will be forever separated from him. God has given us the privilege of being difference makers, so let's use our opportunities to show them God's love for them.

44. "It is more likely for me to be bored out of Christianity than it is for me to be reasoned out of it."

Concerning His Son Jesus Christ our Lord, who was born of the seed of David according to the flesh, and declared to be the Son of God with power according to the Spirit of holiness, by the resurrection from the dead. (Rom. 1:3–4)

There are times a mentor says something that deeply touches you because of something that was going through your mind at the time. Some may question the first part of Dr. Robinson's statement, asking, "What does he mean when he says that being bored out of Christianity is more likely?" I sincerely have no idea. He may have been referring to anything from boring sermons to boring Christians. To me, the first half of the sentence isn't what matters. It was the second part that really impacted me and caught my attention. Dr. Robinson's words struck me because I had been thinking about my coming to Christ. I realized that even though my conversion was a special moment between God and me, I had no one to help me, guide me, or answer any of my questions. As I grew and struggled at the same time, there were moments I wondered how one can be certain this is absolutely right. I believed that Christ was who he said he was. But what if I was wrong? On what basis does all this stand or fall? In retrospect, had it not been for God's sovereign protection of me I could have gotten into some pretty weird theological beliefs.

In my mentorship with Dr. Robinson, he consistently took me back to the resurrection—the one truth on which Christianity either stands or falls. Because of his guidance, I discovered that the empty tomb was the most attested fact of history. In a sense Dr. Robinson was saying, "Be as bored as you want to be with Christianity; you cannot deny the truth behind it." Christianity is based on something that is undeniably true: Jesus Christ rose on the third day. Romans 1:4 became one of my favorite verses. The resurrection proved Christ to be who he was.

Admittedly, parts of the creation story might be hard to believe, as well as other Bible stories such as Jonah and the big fish. The virgin birth and the Trinity are also difficult to explain. But in a way, they are not the issue because they are not the basis on which Christianity stands or falls. If you study the evidence behind the empty tomb, it all makes sense. It is reasonable. Even unbelievers have testified that the one thing they cannot escape is that the resurrection was supernatural. There is no other explanation for it, even if they wish there was. I often quote an agnostic who said, "Let's not talk about the other miracles. Let's talk about the resurrection. If the resurrection is true, every other miracle is true. If the resurrection is not true, no other miracle matters."

Now when I meet someone who has any doubts about the deity of Christ, I challenge them to disprove the resurrection. I have never met one person who studied it objectively who did not come to Christ. And in that Dr. Robinson's words ring true: it is easier to fall out of Christianity from boredom than from questionable facts. The empty tomb does not tell us Christ is the Son of God; it shouts it!

45. "The opposite of faith is not doubt; it is disobedience."

"You search the Scriptures, for in them you think you have eternal life; and these are they which testify of Me. But you are not willing to come to Me that you may have life." (John 5:39–40)

Mentors are not always right, and a good mentor never claims to be. One time, when Dr. Robinson and I were interacting about why some people have an easier time coming to Christ than others, I declared that he was mistaken. It was then that he made the above statement.

Initially, I was skeptical of his words. The opposite of faith is disobedience? I thought to myself, "There is no way. The opposite of faith has to be doubt, right? If I don't believe it, I doubt it." But once again, he drove me to the Scriptures, in particular John 5:39–40. This passage discusses the Jewish leaders who read and studied the Old Testament yet still struggled to accept the truth that the writings show. Though the truth is undeniable, they would not come to the Lord. It was not that they could not believe, but that they would not.

In the past, I would have assumed that they could not believe because of the lack of proper factual evidence or doubt. However, it was the fact that they "are not *willing* to" believe that keeps them from entering into God's presence. In other words, they heard and saw the truth but chose disobedience.

After hearing Dr. Robinson's explanation and digging into Scripture, I began to reflect on all my experiences in evangelism. There are people who meet the Savior and yet turn aside from him because they are unwilling to come to him. Some will not study the prophecies of the Old Testament or the evidence behind the resurrection, and thus are unable to have their eyes opened to the truth. Others study it and reject it, while some look at the facts and respond in faith.

Atheists say, "There is no God." Yet every day they walk in the midst of God's fingerprints: the trees, flowers, clouds, stars. They could accept the facts but they won't. An agnostic says, "I am not sure there is a God." Why not make sure the way millions of others have? The problem is their will, not their mind. A person declares, "My good works will get me to heaven because I have lived a lot better than most people I know." But the Bible says they won't. The issue is rebellion: defiance of what God has declared. A person angrily states, "Don't talk to me about a God of love. Why does he stand there with his arms folded when so many are suffering?" Yet I have never met someone who could say that after seriously studying the cross. Why? Because they chose not to.

A new convert once said to me, "I always thought the problem was with my head until I found out that the problem was with my heart." When I think about that in connection to Dr. Robinson's words, I can see how faith is much more reliant on the condition and openness of a person's heart than a person's mind. When it comes down to it, the heart is where disobedience originates. This is well represented in what an unbeliever once said to me: "I don't think what you are saying is true. Even if it was, I wouldn't accept it. I am too stubborn to do that." What a testimony to the real problem.

That is why, as we evangelize, unbelievers need our patience and our prayers. They *can* believe. The question is, will they open their hearts and respond to his invitation?

Dr. Haddon Robinson (early 1950s)

Dr. Robinson with his Doctor of Ministry
students (around 2012)

Dr. Robinson with son Torrey at his graduation
from Gordon-Conwell Theological Seminary (2001)

Dr. Robinson, Bonnie, and Larry (2008)